Alaska Salmon and Sail

Walter Noden

VANTAGE PRESS
New York

Copyright © 2000 by Walter Noden

Published by Vantage Press, Inc.
516 West 34th Street, New York, New York 10001

Manufactured in the United States of America
ISBN: 0-533-13378-5

Library of Congress Catalog Card No.: 99-97058

0 9 8 7 6 5 4 3 2 1

Thank you to my mother for making me an Alaskan Upiak Native, and to my wife, Florence, for fifty-nine wonderful years.

Contents

Wattamuse to Arolik

My name is Walter Malcolm Noden. I was born to William Malcolm and Annie Noden on January 22, 1919. I am one-half Yupik Alaska Native and one-half Scottish-Irish-English. Here is my story.

In January of the year 1919, my parents walked from Wattamuse to Arolik, Alaska. My mother was already nine months' pregnant and ready to have her baby, and Arolik wasn't the closest village to the mine at Wattamuse. I don't know why they chose Arolik, but maybe there were better trail conditions or my mother could have had her choice in midwives in Arolik. They probably used a small sled to carry some survival items, especially food and sleeping bags. In those days, Alaskan sleeping bags were made out of reindeer hide. They were a little too cumbersome for backpacks. The weather in Alaska was unpredictable and no one in their right mind would ever venture anywhere without survival items.

At the time the dollar was pretty hard to come by. The only way to get a few dollars was through mining or trapping. During the journey to Arolik, my parents were met by a large herd of land otter. When they crossed paths, they stopped to rest and watch the otter. There must have been fifty or more in that migration. My father couldn't get any because he didn't have time to care for the catch. They needed to get to Arolik so my mother could have her baby.

Good News Bay

The first time I remember anything, or felt and saw life on this earth, my mother and father were hugging me, laughing and crying at the same time. My mother later told me that when I was in the crawling/walking stage, I had wandered away and gotten lost. After about an hour of frantic searching, they heard me crying and found me in some deep grass and brush.

I remember waking up and playing with some white puppies. Later on, the puppies grew up to be my white Siberian Huskies: Tom, Dick, Harry, and Joe. The dogs and I grew up together. Somewhere along the line, one dog died, and I only had Tom, Dick, and Joe. I know Harry must have died. Dad never would have sold him.

Another time after I woke up, I was playing with a girl about my age. My dogs were chained to their doghouse. This had to have been Good News Bay in western Alaska. By this time the dogs had grown up enough to require chaining.

Hagemeister

The first time I saw surf on the beach and rocks, I couldn't turn my mind to anything else. It must have been the seal in the water so close to the rocks, that attracted most of my attention because I remembered staying so long at the porthole. Just when I thought for sure he'd gotten dashed on the rocks, he'd pop his head up in another place. I just watched, wondering what he was and why he kept looking at us when he came out of the water. I wonder today what the hell that seal was thinking. He was down wind so he could smell man, but the rest of it was probably pretty new to him, the engine noise and diesel smell.

I forgot all about that seal, when as our boat nudged close to shore, my dad started throwing my dogs overboard. My mother held on to me tightly because I wanted to jump into the water with them.

It wasn't too long before my dad came and put me aboard the skiff we were using to unload. I think I was about five or six at the time and wasn't paying too much attention to what was going on. I found out that we were off-loading our winter trapping supplies from a trading schooner, that my parents had hopped a ride on. It was called *Joe Jeans Trading Boat,* on its way from Good News Bay to Dillingham.

We must have had an unusually calm day because I found out later that any shore waters in the Bering Sea, on a "calm" day, were rough. We got on board the skiff by hanging onto anything we could find and clinging to each other. Through the surf, we found the creek mouth we wanted to hide in. Once we were through the breakers, we found ourselves in a small harbor, which was at the mouth of a stream behind the cliffs. I remember my mother holding me and I was crying pretty damn hard, because my father was throwing the dogs into the water one at a time from the boat anchored near the beach. The dogs were thrown over board to swim ashore. I wanted to jump in with them. All the rest of the stuff was sent over in the skiff that my mother and I had come over in. The skiff was left with us. I guess it must have been ours.

There was already a lot of stuff on the beach; probably everything my dad owned sat on that beach. This was Hagemeister Island and we were to spend the winter there.

The next thing I remember, we were in a little house. To this day I don't know what it was built from. It had to have been driftwood, canvas, or sod. There was a fire in a small sheet iron stove, and for the first time I could remember, I was warm. I have never since been so warm and cozy in my life. I have since been warm, or had almost the same feeling by lying on a sandy warm beach, or with my wife, or drinking with friends, or just saying "hello" to someone. It has never been that same fully contented feeling I had sleeping with my dad and mother under those wool blankets on a reindeer mattress, with the surf making its own music in harmony with the wind whistling over the rocky shore. I wonder who could have awakened me from this. I wonder right this moment, if I could experience this feeling again?

We had established our winter trapping cabin at the mouth of a small stream. There was shelter there because the streambed was much lower than the rest of the backcountry. There were no trees, just bare hills with grass and brush in the lower places. Most of the time, I was able to do as I pleased around the camp. With my three huskies for partners, I didn't realize there were no other children to play with. We were always within sight of home. In the evenings the dogs were chained to their doghouses, and that was the time I had to stay indoors. The huskies must have been guarding me during the day. Wood was stacked on end and made a teepee for the three dogs. The wood must have been driftwood found off the surrounding shore and stacked for the winter.

On the shoreline, when the tide was out, there was sand, with gravel, and boulders of all sizes. Among the boulders were small water pools, which held tiny, moving sea creatures. Sometimes flounder could be found in the larger pools. Mother took the flounder and the black mussels that clung to the boulders. This seafood was a wonderful change from the wild meat that the island provided.

What I liked most about Hagemeister, was when I'd go with my mother to pick mussels. As I remember, there was a spot where these black, oblong mussels clung to the rocks. For me, there were all sorts of new things to fill my pockets with.

There were a lot of red fox on the island. I saw them at times along the beach feeding on sea animals and fish that drifted ashore.

One time there was a dead walrus about a half-mile from us, I knew about this because I could smell it when the wind was right. Once Mother and I walked up to it while picking mussels, it was blown up as big as

5

a blimp. There must not have been too many sales for walrus tusks those years, because my dad didn't even bother with them. Probably wasn't as much of an outside market as there is today.

We lived like the animal we were to trap that winter. There were salmon in the stream. Once they were caught, some were dried for dog food. The better-cared-for salmon was hung separately for us.

The smelt were dried by weaving its head into a rope of strong beach grass. Some were cleaned and gutted, while others were left whole.

My dad salted some of the salmon. They were filleted and then packed in the barrel with salt between each layer. That winter those filets were soaked in water to remove the salt, then boiled. Served with a boiled potato, it made a wonderful hearty meal. The potatoes were kept in a small root cellar that was built into the sandy banks and lined with wood of some kind.

Later that fall, there was a run of trout. They were split the same as the salmon, some carefully cared for and others just slashed down the belly and strung up by their heads to dry. Again, the better-cared-for fish was to be ours, and the rough-cut fish was for the dogs.

I didn't pay much attention to all of this and didn't help much with caring for the fish, except to carry the water for cleaning some of this fish and for our cabin. This lasted for one trip because Mother wanted more than one cup of water at a time.

The fish rack had a tarp over the top because it rained a lot. As soon as one batch dried, it was stuffed into gunnysacks and taken to the cache.

This food cache was a driftwood and canvas affair. It stood on four posts about five feet off the ground. It had tin can lengths wrapped around each post so mice and other small animals couldn't get up to it. Suffice to say the ladder was fixed up the same way.

My mother and I took care of the fishing business. Dad was the hunter. There were geese, ducks, and cranes. Dad got mostly geese, possibly because of the scarcity of ammunition. Besides that, my mother had her own way of catching the ducks.

There was a small indentation in the creek shore where the ducks liked to swim into. My mother made a duck trap there. I've never seen a more efficient contraption for catching ducks, since then.

The narrow part of the creek was probably about twelve feet wide. About halfway across this, we planted willows close together on the bottom. From the other side, we placed a stick high enough so the birds could swim under it. From this, she hung snares made of animal hide or sinew, I don't know which. The snares were then held into place by grass tied to two small sticks, one on each side. Each morning there was a duck or two. This was close to the cabin so the birds didn't come there during the day, only early mornings when things were quiet.

The ducks were dried the same as everything else. Some were carefully plucked and cleaned, others were skinned and not cared for so well. Like the fish, some were for us and some were for the dogs. The skinned ones were fish duck. Some ducks, I believe they were shags, were carefully skinned with the feathers on.

Then they were turned inside out, stuffed with grass, and hung up to dry.

I found out that winter why this certain duck was dried then tanned. My mother made long coats from it. The duck provided the whole coat. The thread came from the sinew in the duck's legs. I don't know how the duck was tanned, but I know my coat was soft and warm. The feathers were on the outside, so I felt like a walking duck in it. Our coats, when not in use, were always hung in the cabin when the weather was damp or wet, and outside when the weather and wind permitted.

I think about my down-filled coat today, made by a white man in Seattle, who plucked the bird first, then stuffed the feathers into it. Nature put the feathers on my other coat, which served as a down coat, a windbreaker, and a raincoat. I often thought I'd like one today, but I probably would not know how to care for it. Besides, I'd probably be arrested for catching the duck and called a cuckoo for wearing it.

I slept in a deer hide sleeping bag. In wintertime, when the cabin was cold at night, I stayed toastie warm because the fur was on the inside. During warmer weather, it was used as a mattress with the fur side out.

It sure wasn't made for backpackers, though. It was a pretty large bundle and hard to carry. However, one of these bags was always carried in my dad's sled. All the teams had a sleeping bag with them. There was no telling when a team would get stranded in a winter storm.

Much of the discarded fish and seal that was unfit

for dog food was separated and buried in different places. It may have been my mother's belief that the fish did not want to be buried with his enemy, the seal.

All this was in one particular area. I think it was to be used as a gardening site.

Later, we picked cranberries and salmon berries there. All these berries grew in the tundra, all on short stalks no more than two inches off the ground. The salmon berries were smaller than the berries that grow on bushes as they do in warmer parts of Alaska. They were not as plentiful as the other berries either.

Our little bay—for that's what I'll call it—provided enough shelter from the storms so that we were always comfortable during stormy weather. The cliffs that had been formed by the stream mostly provided the shelter. The spot was also in a small bay itself. It was a good spot, for the stream provided fresh water, driftwood, sea animals, and birds.

During the times we had to stay indoors, my mother sewed most of the time, and Dad, being a tinsmith, made many useful things from tin and metal saved from the containers that drifted ashore. He, also, made small parts for the dog sled that was being built out of doors.

He could, also, do some rough sewing. I know he made his own dog harness. These were very simply constructed. They were simply long tubes of sewn canvas, something like a fire hose. Inside these were placed strands of old manila rope that must have been thrown overboard by a sailing ship. The strands were tied to one end of the canvas tube, and the canvas tube was rolled outside in over the strands. The canvas tube wound up with the sewn part inside with the rope strands. The harness was in two parts; one part went around the neck, sewn together and under his front legs, continued on back and over the rump. Then one rope and canvas strap was connected to the top of the collar and continued back to meet the other two at the tail end. There was a snap a little past this junction.

We built an addition to the cabin that fall. It was smaller than our living quarters. Although neither one was very large, it was where we stretched and dried the fox, and dried the dog harnesses that winter. There was a smaller stove in the addition (both were of tin) and this was lit during the day, I believe, at least once.

That winter, my dad and the dogs were gone most of the day. The dogs pulled the sled with the necessary gear. He would walk behind the sled sometimes, but after a fresh snow, he walked in front with snowshoes on.

Sometimes he came home with one or more foxes and at others times there were none. We met them at the hitching post. Mother unloaded the sled, while Dad unhitched the dogs.

The dogs didn't jump around and try to play with me at these homecomings. Instead, they went right under the woodpile teepee. They were fed one dried fish and a small piece of seal fat; I believe they got the fat about twice a week.

So, I was left as an unobserved spectator.

My dad had steel traps, but he, also, used poison. He had a small cache where the poisoned bait was kept.

I know this because I was never allowed anywhere near that cache. This was sometime between 1925 and 1927, and I'm sure that he was not the only one in those days to do this.

Alaska was very badly exploited back then. Not by my mother's Yupik Native race but by my father's white one. The white man poisoned animals when it was advantageous and used the native population in a shameful manner. There was not much difference there from the Lower 48 when the Indians were nearly exterminated along with the buffalo by such heroes as Buffalo Bill.

The winter was not as memorable to me as summer. I was not outside as much as I was in summer. My dogs were grown-up sled dogs by now, so most of their home time was used to eat, sleep, and rest. They had pulled their sleds for most of the day. Mother too, rested in bed with my dad. She did have home chores, such as to gather and chop wood, chop open the frozen well to carry water home, to clean the cabin, and to cook. There were, I'm sure, set days for her to cook dog meals. This was special fat food, such as boiled dried seal meat.

Then she had her only baby to bathe. Those days went against my grain. The water was wet, the soap was soapy in my eyes, and I thought the whole damn idea was unreasonable.

There is, I believe, a rule in life—if there is dark, then there must come light.

And there was.

The sun came for its summer visit.

When spring arrived and it became warmer outdoors, Mom would take me out in the snow. And to me, the snow was never cold when the sun visited.

Mom had a native story knife. It's a piece of ivory the shape of a knife with a dull blade. Mom carved pictures on the melting snow to tell me stories that her mother had told to her. She would do this every chance we had together that spring.

Some of the stories would be about us; others would be about different things.

I saw pictures of a bear attacking a kayak, of a kayak in a storm. Of a rabbit that ran to lead a bear away from his family.

She made snow pictures of a tundra rabbit dance. All of the rabbits were dancing in circles on the snow. The male rabbits danced around the female rabbits in the picture.

Now, those old "story knives" are on display at most museums in Alaska.

Mickey Mouse is doing the same thing today in the daily funnies. I, myself, today subscribe to our paper, not for the headlines I saw on TV about murder or war, but because of my Alaska Native mother's native "funnies on snow."

And the very first thing I do in the morning is open the paper to the funnies!

Ekuk

Village Life

Spring-move.

Sometime after the snow left, the same trader came and we were all ready and went with the boat. We moved to the village of Ekuk, next to a salmon cannery, named "Libby's Ekuk Cannery."

Ekuk was a small village, but it was the first place I saw with more than two houses next to each other. The houses were stretched out along the Nushagak shoreline for about two and a half or three miles as it is today.

I could count everything. There was the cannery watchman's, and twelve family homes of mixed nationalities. There was Alaska/Native, Japanese/Native, and White/Native. Mine was Alaska/Native from my mother and Scottish-Irish-English from my father.

The only "law" Ekuk had was in Dillingham, twenty miles up the Nushagak River. This "law" consisted of one judge or commissioner and one U.S. marshal.

There were very few residential people in the area. At the "bluff end," there was the Pallagan's house, Nick Nauken's house, our house (Shorty Nutten's), and Jimmy's house. Towards the cannery, about two miles away was Joe's house, Pete's house, and Johnny's house.

So, Ekuk consisted of men who were immigrants. There were Japanese, Filipinos, and Scots. In turn, some were married to Alaska native women. The families got along well together, as did all the villages in those days.

All the kids played together during nice weather and ate at different houses throughout the day. In the evenings we were herded to our own homes.

There were two girls, Hanna and Polaska (which was changed to Alaska by a teacher at the school in Clark's.) The boys included Mike, Pete, Johnny, Joe, Frank, Jimmy, and me.

I remember some of our play times.

For instance, while at play we accidentally set fire to the grass between the cannery and Jimmy's house. We were all scared and hiding in the grass. There were a couple of Chinese men who came to investigate.

We teased the Chinese workers whenever we could sneak into the cannery. We stole their nails and did whatever we could do to aggravate them.

The bluffs going from Cape Etolin to Ekuk are on average between fifteen to twenty feet high. These bluffs left the shoreline at Ekuk and turned forty-five degrees to the north, continuing to Clark's Point about three miles north. This left a fairly large swamp between the shoreline and the bluffs about a mile from the beach. It was about three miles long and located between the village and the cannery. It was here that all of us kids played. Of course, we were restricted from going to the swamp. Probably because of the bad swamp holes, but it didn't stop us.

We played most of the English games kids play today. We were different in only one way: we made our own play boats, bats, balls, and skates. We nailed together scows from pieces of sheet iron and rowed around in the swamps and ponds behind the village. These things stayed afloat no more than five minutes to a voyage, but they had captains and crew just like the cannery boats. We never built rafts because we'd never seen one.

We made our ice skates by splitting a wooden net float in half, then hammering a piece of tin or discarded sled runner to it. This was strapped to our shoes with pieces of net twine. The skates worked, but today I'll be damned if I know how.

We had never seen a baseball game, but we played a game called Mi'atchee that was very similar. We only had two bases, home and first base, about fifty feet apart. Instead of throwing the ball to the catcher, we threw the ball straight in the air in front of the bat. When the ball was hit, we ran to first base, but there was no first baseman. Anyone from the opposing team would get the ball any way he could and try to hit the runner with it. There was a little discomfort if you were hit in the wrong place, or if you were hit in the head or face with a wet muddy ball made of rags wrapped with net twine. We had no ump, so I think the best part of the game came when deciding who won, These decisions caused the largest amount of sore spots and nosebleeds.

The girls joined in on hide and seek. We boys didn't do much of that, but I remember hiding with one of the girls and I got her panties off, but I didn't know what to do after that. Of course there were slingshot hunting parties. I don't believe that there was ever one living creature hit on these hunts.

Winter was for "one dog" sleds and barrel slides, with skis made from old barrel staves with foot straps made of seal skin, not leather.

That summer Dad fished. We had two set nets. There were two types of fishing. A lot of the salmon were fished by sailboat, then there were the set nets. The set nets were up to three hundred feet long and were stretched out on the gravel beach between two anchors or stakes. They caught the fish as the tide came in and the fish were picked out as the tide went out. The fish were taken to the cannery by Model T trucks.

When I first saw one of these monsters, I didn't know what the hell the thing was. You can imagine seeing me, an Alaskan Native kid about eight years old, in that tall grass just at eye level and one of Henry Ford's monsters comes charging through that grass right at you. You wouldn't have time to shit your pants because you would have been too busy running for your life. I was both scared and very curious. It wasn't long before I got friendly with the beast and every chance I had, I would climb aboard. That incident was probably my initiation into this modern world and its style.

Cannery Operation

Later on that summer, other boys and I would sneak into the cannery and try to start these trucks. See, that truck was the center of attraction for the Ekuk kids. We all knew that we were to stay well away from it, but neither the driver nor our parents knew we would inspect it when the opportunity presented itself.

There were Jitneys, besides the Model T. They were used to tow the canned salmon in large four-wheeled carts from the retort to the cooling area, and from the cooling area to labeling, and from there to the docks. These were, then, loaded on a scow.

The scow was a wooden barge, a square thing about fifty by twenty and the cases were taken to a waiting ship. It was the steam ship *W. C. Gorcas*. This was about 1927 to 1928; and the state was a territory then.

Alaska was owned by the United States government and exploited by the cannery owners. The steamships would come in the springtime; it must have been the end of May. The ship would blow its whistle three times and drop anchor, then the all white beach gang would come ashore. They had all their own stuff: bunkhouse, cook, everything. They even had their own donkey boiler to make steam for the winch that launched the monkey boats and barges from the winter storage way at the cannery.

The monkey boat was a small diesel-powered tugboat. Right after that came the barge, this unit (a small tug and barge) went immediately to the ship. There were more barges than monkey boats, but that's how it worked. Most tugs had big two-cylinder diesels. Seemed to me, they were mostly flywheel. The flywheel had about a one hundred-horse diesel. I remember it had holes that fit an iron bar. The engineer started the thing by turning the wheel with this iron bar. The engine would build up air pressure once it had first been started; and it could be started with the stored air after that. There was a priority system: first the beach gang, cooks, longshoremen, next the fishermen. The fishermen were either Norwegian or Italian. The cannery would have one or the other, either all Norwegian or all Greek. Must have been because of communication problems. The last to come off were the Chinese and Filipino gangs, they were the cannery workers.

Libby's had two twelve-hour shifts for the cannery workers. There was a "Filipino boss" and a "China boss." Every gang or group had its own bunkhouse. China bunkhouse, fishermen, cooks, beach gang and so on. They, also, had different mess halls and cooks, white cookhouse and oriental cookhouse.

The food was dried, salted, or canned. There were enough pigs to clean up the leftovers from the mess halls. The vegetables were stored in big root cellars. Ice was also stored in these sod-covered storages. The ice was stored in big blocks during the winter, with sawdust, probably so it would not freeze together.

The canneries were run by steam. The steam was generated in large high-pressure steam boilers, then piped to different places in the cannery. The steam engines were belted to overhead shafts, which distributed power to different canning machines. Steam was also used in the cooking retorts, for cleaning and in wash areas.

During the time the canneries were in, I don't remember much of anything but tending to the nets. After they left, it was different.

When they left they took everything with them. The canned fish was the first aboard ship. Then all the boats were hauled up and stored in the cannery. After that, the ship took off and all the people with it. I don't know why it gave three whistles because I know they didn't care enough for the locals to say "so-long." The whistles must have been for the cannery itself, and the cannery watchman.

The watchman was a year-round worker, "beach boss" during the summer and watchman during the winter. The beach boss and his "beach gang" took care of all the barges, docks, tugs and boat haul-ups. They also ran and maintained all the steam winches and pile drivers. Then there were the carpenters and their "carpenter boss."

It wasn't too long before we were big enough to help with the set nets. We helped pack the salmon for carrying up the beach to a pile where they were washed of gravel and mud. Then they were put in a pile for the truck that brought them to the cannery.

On Sundays, we helped put up dried fish for dog food and personal winter food. We had to guard the salmon because the seagulls would get through the protective netting and get to the fish. We were constantly fixing the nets and rehanging fish. No matter what we did, they seemed to get through all the time. I still hate seagulls to this day.

I remember there was this old blind man who stayed at the Pallagen house. I used to go there and watch him carve ivory. He would take a piece of ivory, feel it all over and then knick it with his carving knife, and then feel the knick. The next day he would start carving. His knife was half-moon shaped, with an ivory handle. He made ladies trinkets, spearheads, arrowheads, rings, etc. . . . He'd always show them to me when he was finished. If someone in the village wanted something made, they brought it to him and he would duplicate it in ivory.

The Flood

We lived in Ekuk until the flood. It came in the fall of 1929 or 1930, after the cannery shut down. The floodwaters came quick. All of a sudden, there was water everywhere. It cleaned out the village, except for two houses that were on the hillside. Everyone clustered around these houses and took turns in them. The waves were as big as the houses that were being smashed.

I'll never forget this husky dog rescuing her pups. She would dive into those big waves and, after what seemed like a long time but was probably only a minute or less, she would come rolling in with a pup by the neck. I know she had five, and she only got three of them that way; the fourth try was a failure. After that she started moving those three to higher ground. I stopped watching because I was frozen stiff. She put those puppies close to me as if she were asking me to care of them if she didn't come out of those waves.

The next day the flat land behind the village was covered with everything imaginable, houses, lumber, boats . . .

Dillingham

The government moved us to a bigger village called Dillingham that winter and I went to school. I don't remember too much about this school, except I didn't like it.

Our cabin was close to the beach and the bank of the Nushagak River. My dad spent the winter doing odd jobs and making camp stoves for the trappers.

He made his own homebrew too. He was very good at it. The still was always dripping into a jar. Cash was hard to come by, so the old guys would trade something for Dad's brew and white lightning. He must have gotten some cash to buy the sugar he used or else he traded for it. I'm not sure which.

Back to Ekuk

We ended up in Ekuk the next spring to tend our

set nets. It must have been the spring of 1930. The cannery helped people move their houses back. Some of the houses were in pieces, but were made livable. The cannery carpenter did the work. I believe there was no charge for his work.

The only hard money them days came from salmon and fur. The furs were mostly beaver and fox. In the order of dollar value: salmon, beaver, and fox.

That summer I was old enough to help with the fishing. My dad was sick most of the time. He died in the summer of 1930. So I did most of the work on the nets. We got through the fishing season somehow.

Mom and I had work to do, so I didn't have much association with the boys of the village. We had to put up the dried fish for Tom, Dick, and Joe, my three Siberian huskies. We gathered driftwood for winter.

During the summer the dogs ate mostly fresh cooked fish. All of the fish was used, except for the very sharp teeth. I believe this is what kept the dogs so healthy. There were probably enough minerals and needed vitamins in the different parts of the fish to keep the dogs clean-coated and healthy. During winter they ate dried fish.

I went ground squirrel hunting with my mom. We had a tent probably about three miles from the village and took care of our squirrel snares from this base camp.

The Alaska parka squirrel is a fat little guy, about a foot long. We made the snares out of picture-hanging wire. They used to use sinew, but I guess times change. The snare was placed inside the mouth of the squirrel hole. It had a small stick tied right above the snare circle, which was put through a hole from the outside into the tunnel; then a small V branch was placed at the bottom of the hole inside the tunnel. The end of the snare was tied to a spring willow, the straight stick was placed across the small part of the V stick, and the snare end tied to willow branch.

When the squirrel got snared, he started to struggle and activated the willow spring business, and was choked to death. The squirrel died quickly, the meat and hide were better with a quick death. The squirrel was skinned, cleaned, and gutted. The meat was dried with the legs hanging down and a piece of braided grass around his neck. The skin was turned inside out, stuffed with grass and hung up by the nose to dry.

Another trip I remember going on was a mouse food-gathering trip.

Field mice were abundant along the edge of the swamp. It was dry and grassy with berries and many different kinds of plants. The mice would store winter food in the fall.

Mom knew the right time to get a certain root she wanted. She'd find a good area and walk using short steps and a sort of stomping as she moved. Once she found an underground storage area, she would carefully cut the top off with her ulu knife and lift it off. There would be rooms full of roots, berries, very small wild onions, and other unknown mouse food, each stored according to food type.

Mother just wanted the root. It was oblong, dark brown to black, and about one inch long and a quarter inch in diameter. She, then, replaced the roots with raisins and carefully put the top back on. I don't remember ever eating more than one piece of mouse food.

I'm sure my mother had a reason for this. Was it because she wanted the mouse food or was it to teach me something about the caring native way?

When I think back on this, I believe my mother was trying to teach me something her mother taught to her: "Care for nature and nature will care for you."

Squaw Creek

Mom and I moved back to Dillingham soon after Dad's death. There she met Billy Anderson and after a while got remarried. I became one in a family of four boys and two girls.

We lived at Squaw Creek, which was three miles from Dillingham. We went to school there. We walked to school before the snow and used a dog team when there was enough snow.

The school we went to had one teacher up until I passed eighth grade, when some of us students ended up with a husband-and-wife team, who taught high school.

In the 1936–37 school year, I was already fishing in a boat as a partner.

The winter of the 1937–38 school year, the two teachers and four of us high school kids got together to study high school subjects in the attic of the grade school.

The man taught us two boys and two girls math and history. His wife taught typing and English. I had a tough time with the typing because my hands were so big. I passed just by a hair. I typed 71 words.

These classes helped because us two boys went to *Annacoats High* in Washington. The school gave us credit for the subjects we took at the school in Dillingham. The husband-and-wife team had sent a packet with the two of us containing our grades and a letter.

My dogs, Tom, Dick, and Joe, would not let the rest of the family handle them, so I took care of them myself. As for the rest of the dogs (there was nine in all), Nels and I fed them one dried fish a day. When the weather was decent, we cooked for them. The dogs' cook pot was an oil drum cut in half. In it we would cook cut up dried fish, flour, and/or corn meal that had spoiled, and water. It made one hell of a smelly stew. It was cooked out of doors over a wood fire. After a long trip or when we were hauling wood, the dogs got a ration of tallow.

We were two older boys and two younger boys. The older boys cut the wood in the fall and stacked it in the woods to wait for snow to haul it home. Once it was home, they cut it up and split it. We younger boys packed it to the woodshed and stacked it. In the meantime, we were burning last year's wood.

We, also, carried out all the slop waters and trash, and carried fresh water from the spring. The water detail was when I first remember thinking, *why is it always up hill?* Why wasn't the spring higher, so we didn't have to push a loaded sled uphill? I'm just beginning to find out everyone has a hill to climb before he can have the downhill.

My stepfather was strict but fair. The two of us got twenty-five cents a week to spend in town where there were silent movies, candy, and other good things on Saturday.

I, also, got a little extra money as a bootlegger's helper. I gathered empty bottles for the local bootlegger and got ten cents a bottle. I was the richest kid around when it was bottling time. One time, I remember finding five bottles. I had fifty cents all at one time right in my hand.

This was during the Prohibition Era. Anyone who wanted beer or whiskey, and didn't make it himself, had to buy it from the local bootlegger.

The local officials (the commissioner, he was the judge and the marshal; he was the police) bought bootlegger booze too. Indirectly, of course.

Thinking back on this, I don't remember hearing of a white man being arrested for alcohol possession. It was always the Yupik native who was arrested and fined.

I believe that the commissioner kept the fines, or at least a portion of them, for his commission. I believe that the marshal was paid for feeding the prisoners, so he got his share.

Dog Driving

During the dog-driving season, I started training our dogs. I started the training program by accident. All the dogs were gone one day and being in a bit of a hurry, I put their food next to each dog house. When the nine dogs got home and were being unhitched, I noticed each one would fight to get to his dog house. We used to have to unhitch each dog and take him to his place in the chain. This process was time-consuming and a lot of extra work, which no one needed. So, when I saw this happen, the little bell start ringing—sure put the food there and they'll go home. No more dragging them to the chain while they were trying to make side trips.

I tried it and, sure enough, as I unharnessed them, each dog would run home and start eating. And all I had to do was walk from dog house to dog house and snap on the chain. It wasn't too long before they would run to their houses even when there was no food. They knew that food was coming, so going home to the dog house became easy.

Our lead dog, Rusty, was about half as big as the rest of the team, but they didn't fight him because they knew they'd get the chain. It was a common practice to use a dog chain to stop dog fights. A lot of our dogs had some wolf in them and they could cripple each other in a fight if left alone—even kill each other. I never had to use the chain very often because I lived with them—feeding, watering, and changing the grass in their houses.

The dogs were all obedient to my command, if they understood my wish. All I had to do was shout to stop a fight. Sometimes, when there were more than two dogs involved, I would just dive right in with them. They would stop and cower. They didn't seem to know that anyone of them could take one rip and I'd be gone.

I thought about this later on in life. What the hell was I doing in a "wolf dog-fight-to-the-finish?"

There was a time when I had to jump in and save one of my older step-brothers, Johnny, from my Huskies.

See, John had hitched up my dogs, Tom, Dick, and Joe along with four others, to make a seven-dog team. Katie, one of my stepsisters, came charging into the house yelling, "Walter! Your dogs are killing Johnny!"

I ran out and saw that all three of my dogs were on him. I never hesitated. I jumped in yelling and stopped the fighting.

The only way I can figure out how this fight started was that Johnny must have used a chain on them. It was a *very* good thing that he had been wearing heavy winter clothes, or else the dogs would have torn him up.

We unhitched the dogs because now Johnny was too sick to go on his "booze run" that night.

Beaver Trapping

About the end of April, we would have to leave school and go beaver trapping. Everyone was allowed ten beavers as a limit. Eight people, eight limits. So a limit of ten pelts at thirty-dollars a pelt was good. We also fished for six cents a fish, not per pound. We started trapping through the ice. The beaver houses were already located in the fall before the snow covered them. The beavers made feed piles of willow underwater. The beaver snares were set near the feed piles. The fresh willows or aspen we put in would always bring them to the snare.

We didn't concentrate too much on catching them through the ice because after spring breakup we could get them without chopping ice. The breakup came around the middle of May, or a little before that. Breakup was a time of grinding ice jams and floodwater. First the larger creeks and small rivers filled full of water. This was up on the higher ground and covered the beaver houses.

We were there at the head of one of these streams with a canoe. We brought the canoe in by dog team over high ground then sent the team home. See, the dogs would go to the main camp if they were turned loose and not fed.

We drifted down and shot the larger beaver with .22 Special or .22 Long Rifle. A drift usually took about two or three days. When we got enough for the day, we made camp and rough-skinned the beaver and hung the meat in a tree. By the time we got to the main river, it was also flooded and we could canoe to the cabin. Everybody had a trapping cabin through the woods. We didn't use the river because of ice jams and rough currents.

In camp, we ate as if it were a race to see who could eat the most and the fastest. We'd been living on boiled beaver and that spring goose sure was good. I can taste those meals today, pot-roast goose with rice, bread, and coffee.

Then came the count. The beavers were graded: blanket, extra-large, large, medium, small, and kit. We never sold the small or kit pelts. They where made into fur caps, mitts, and beaver coats.

We didn't hunt during breakup because it was actually very dangerous. The river ran very swiftly, loaded with big and small chunks of ice. Once the river settled down, we set traps on the riverbanks. The traps were set near a place where the beaver already came ashore to cut aspen; or sometimes they were set in any place they could come ashore. When they smelled the bait: beaver caster, which was made up of beaver testicles, they would come ashore every time.

They always would pick a depression along the bank to haul themselves out. The trap was set underwater. I think mostly so they couldn't smell it. A rock tied to the trap chain drowned them after they were caught.

This time of year was fun for me. Us boys did nothing but hunt. We didn't have to leave so early in the morning, but there was an incentive. We got to keep the muskrats we trapped.

The trap line we could do in half a day, but we left right after breakfast. Canoeing from trap to trap was the way we hunted muskrats. We got them with 22 shorts. The beauty of our "rat" business was they were skinned and stretched along with the beaver. I think I pitied the camp people; my mother, stepdad, and the girls. They skinned, cooked, slopped, and did everything else at camp.

Just before dusk we'd head back to camp. Evening was when the beaver came out. My stepbrother and I had a .22 Special and .22 Winchester. We used shorts in the Winchester for the rats and the Special for the beaver. We took turns in front of the canoe with the two rifles. If we got two rats or one beaver, we'd trade places. The one in the back paddled.

I think about those rats today. We two boys got to keep the rats we caught. I know the way America works. We had incentive.

When we all got our limit, we went down river where they were tagged by the game warden and sold along with other rats. We smaller boys were never given our rat money in cash. It was set aside, but we could pick out anything we wanted from the Sears catalog.

Family Fishing

Then it was fishing time again.

Before fishing, we would plant the garden with potatoes, rutabagas, and turnips. Goddamn, I knew about slavery before I saw a black. There was no rototiller, no plow. Just two shovels. We turned over the garden one shovelful at a time. Then we planted those damn potatoes. In the fall it was the same thing. We had to dig them out, dry them, and pack them to the root cellar. I wonder today if I wasn't the inventor of the thought *why me?*

Spring preparation, including our move to our set net sites, was very tedious. Mending and hanging the salmon gill nets was a bad one. But again, there was the incentive. We got fifty cents on Saturday instead of twenty-five cents.

I liked the times when we got the boat ready. If we would paint and launch the boat, we could use it to go to town. That is, if we could get the engine to run.

The gas engine had one cylinder. The carburetor was just a bowl with a float and gravity feed, because I know that there was no fuel pump. The only thing mechanical about the carburetor was the float and needle valve. The flywheel was almost as big as the machine itself. You had to be sure the spark advance was set right, so the damn thing didn't backfire and rip your arm off when you turned the flywheel. Once the thing got going, it was quiet and never quit until you disconnected the wire to the magneto. I think it was quiet because I don't think it turned more than five hundred RPM and the exhaust was under water. There was no keel cooler like the boats today have. Instead it pumped water with a piston pump, through the beast and out the exhaust pipe. The water deadened the exhaust noise and by the time everything came out the exhaust pipe, it was turned to steam.

Boy, what a wonderful boat— no sail, didn't have to row, and you could buck tide, right next to the beach.

I believe there is too much text and not enough practicals today. After you turned a flywheel for an hour, the damn thing wouldn't start and the old man came to say, "This is gasoline, see? You turn the gas tank on first with this valve!" When you learn most of it by yourself, then it's hard to forget. Feed the dogs, pet them—turn the ignition on, then the damn thing will start. I'll never forget my first encounter with a reciprocating internal combustion engine.

Out of the House

My stepdad didn't believe in school beyond the three R's, so I left home to go to the Attic Hi, a small hotel in town. I made a deal with the owner of the hotel to stay there and work for my room and board. I had two bunks in my room, so I talked a friend of mine into staying there. The place had eight other rooms, each with two beds. There was a restaurant, with beer and wine. There was also a small building behind the hotel called "The Snake House." This was where the roughest ones stayed.

The first time we cleaned the place out was after a week-long party had taken its course. I knew we had to do something. We each took two buckets of hot water mixed with lye and soap. We opened the door and threw in the water, buckets and all. Then, we ran like hell. After a while, we could walk into the place and mop it out. There were no sheets in those rooms, so we never bothered with the beds.

We tried cleaning with gasoline one time, but we got caught. Somebody was sober enough to smell the gas. We washed dishes, swept, mopped, made beds, filled the wine bottles from the wine barrels, shoveled snow, and it wasn't long before we became the wine guards. The owners had special wine for themselves.

We didn't realize it at the time, but the wine we took a liking to was very special. We sampled all the stock and the stuff we liked the best was bubbly. It was in grass baskets, with the bottleneck sticking out one end. Then we got called on and told that someone was stealing this wine. We were asked to guard it very closely so no more wine would be stolen. We decided the beer was almost as bubbly. No more wine got stolen and no more was said about it.

Fishing

Roy

After school let out for summer vacation, I went to the cannery where my dad used to sell fish. When I asked for a job, the superintendent told me that I was too young. I didn't know what to do, so I hung around with the fishermen. I stayed in the fishermen's bunkhouse and ate with them. I was watching the guys work when the superintendent came by and said, "Say, young fellow, you'd better get to work right now, or you'll lose your run money." I sure hopped right to it because I knew I was hired.

The fisherman's contract called for them to unload the ship's cargo in the spring and load salmon in the fall. It was known as "run money."

I was given a boat and told to find a partner. One day, along comes this old guy who says he just came from the office, where he was told we were to fish together. His name was Roy.

Roy had come to Libby's Ekuk in a halibut dory with a little one-cylinder put-put in it. He had been prospecting in the Nanek- Kvichak area.

He made sure we shared our boat work together.

Some older fishermen would insist that the young guy do most of the work on the boat himself.

We had some leisure time before the season started. A young guy and I were talking about a poker game in the village. We were talking about possibly going there and maybe getting lucky.

Roy, he sat down with us. He told us about poker and luck. I was old enough to understand that I most likely would have lost my $150 beaver-trapping money. He made sure we understood that luck had nothing to do with winning a poker game.

My old partner was okay except he had some real funny ideas about the way to do some of the work. All the other boats would use their sails to set their nets out, if there was any wind at all. Us, we let the sail down and I would row while he would let the net out.

One day he pointed into the wind and said, "Row that way!"

That's when I turned into a mule. Imagine rowing a water-soaked, twenty-seven-foot fishing boat into the wind. I told him I didn't know who the captain was, because I was given the boat first, but he was older. I was going to the cannery to find out.

After some more words, he said, "OK, I'll row sometime."

I said, "No, we use the sail."

It was so much easier sailing while we both set the net out. Getting the net back in was something else.

Our boat was called a Columbia riverboat. It was about twenty-seven feet long and eight feet wide. Draft about sixteen inches. It was made out of one inch port-

or fordcedar, on oak ribs. The only difference between the bow and stem was the bow was a little higher, and decked in to about three and a half feet back. All of our clothes and bedding were under this deck. We lived in a small tent that was pitched from the bow aft, over the forecastle, to the first touart. Under this cross beam was our grub and cooking gear.

We had a net roller in the stem. It was a cylinder about eight inches by forty inches, and made from wooden slats.

We had three fifty-fathom shackles of net, for a total of nine hundred feet. At times the nets held two thousand fish. It was quite a chore getting that many fish on board. Most times the limit was thirteen hundred fish. The high boats caught their limit every day. Us, one "old fart" and a kid, we missed out sometimes.

Compared to this day, the conditions we fished under were unimaginable. We fished six days a week for one month. From about the twenty-fifth of June till about the twenty-fifth of July.

We had to deliver our fish at least once every twenty-four hours.

There was not one ounce of machinery on those boats. We sailed or rowed wherever we went, we pulled net and weighed anchor by muscle, we bailed water, and had to throw the fish one at a time with a pew, onto a barge that was eight feet above us. Most of these were seven-pound fish, and by the time you pitched your share of the delivery, well, you pitched your share of the delivery!

Today with radar, depth finders, loran C's, GPS,

and four hundred horses, sandbars are no problem. But in a sailboat with only a pike pole to feel for the water depth, and a pair of oars, those sandbars were killers. The difference today is a thirty-two foot fiber glass boat about twelve to fourteen feet wide with a nice cabin, power steering, running water, galley sink, bath, oil stove, fridge, hydraulic rollers, anchor winch, and two three-hundred horsepower diesels.

The Sailor

After Roy, I had a sailor that came off the *Alaska Steam*. He was crazy. One time we went on the beach unintentionally. A storm was just building up, and it was on the ebb, so we didn't lose our load. We were worried about losing the fish. It was almost low water when we grounded. The tide barely left the boat when it started back in.

There was a strong onshore wind. The waves were large enough to set the boat crosswise on the beach and sink it right there.

The sailor said, "How can we save our damn fish?"

Me: "We can't, except if we can put the anchor out with all the line and that's impossible."

Sailor: "Like hell it's impossible. I can walk out there with the anchor."

Me: "Bullshit!"

Sailor: "Watch me."

He took his boots off, jumped over the side of the boat, and asked me to pass the anchor to him! He started walking out into the surf and after twenty fathoms of anchor line got tight, he popped out of the water and swam ashore.

When the boat was almost afloat, we kept the bow into the surf with our backs to it until it floated and the incoming tide swung it into the current.

After we were under sail, the sailor went and dug into his stuff and pulled out a pint. He drank half of it and handed me the rest. So, my first real good drink of hard whiskey was a half, pint of *Old Crow*.

We were soaked and cold as hell. The sailor suggested that we change clothes, but I reminded him that we needed to deliver our catch and that we were late.

After we delivered, the sailor said, "I don't know if I'm wet from sweat or wet from water."

Me: "The outside of my clothes are dry. Do you got another of those bottles?"

Sailor: "Yeah. I have half a case."

Me: "Let's go fishing! To hell with our clothes."

We did change after we set our nets because the salty clothes were a little itchy. We passed out for a few hours on that drift.

Dennis

Dennis and I went to the Territorial School of Mines together.

When school let out for summer vacation, we went to "Libby's Ekuk" to get ready to fish that season together. That season was one of the big seasons for the Nushigak District of Bristol Bay.

Libby McNeil and Libby had a somewhat discriminative attitude towards its resident fisherman. On their bulletin board, they had the Hi boats listed as "outside fishermen-Hi boats" and the resident fishermen as "Hi boat." Dennis and I were listed as "Resident Hi" for most of that season.

It was all a pure accident.

All the boats were ashore for Sunday closure. On Monday, when the fishing started for the week, we noticed that our boat was a little too high on shore. We were the last ones off the beach. Everybody else had drifted upriver on the flood.

This was Dennis's very first fishing season ever and he would always want to sail the boat. I never argued with him about it.

When we got moving, he asked, "Now what?"

"Sail out toward the cape until you see a fish jump," I said, just to get him off my back.

There was no damn fish and I wanted to take a nap while he sailed. To where? I did not care.

I had slept for a couple of hours when Dennis came and woke me up.

"Hey! I've seen a jumper!" he replied.

We were pretty close to Cape Elton and fish were jumping everywhere I looked. I thought, *God bless you—you little white-man angel.*

I said, "I'll take the tiller. Just start throwing the nets out."

We put out three of our fifty-fathom nets. There

wasn't another ship in sight and I rejoiced. This was just so perfect.

We delivered a load before the cannery put on a 1,200-fish limit. We were Resident-Hi for most of that season. The limit stayed on for most of that season too. Every day we caught the same limit as the rest. There was no way they could catch up to us.

Some of the resident fishermen were noticeably sore. I knew why—the resident fishermen from the other canneries were making remarks like "Those kids still hi-boat at your cannery?"

Another thing was that we were allowed to eat in the "Blue Room" where the superintendent and all the bigwigs ate. I ate there once. Dennis ate there every Sunday when we ate ashore.

Once he came out of the Blue Room with a lit cigar in his hand and said, "Hello, boys. How's everything going today?"

I thought I'd better tell him that if he didn't cut it out he might get hurt—told him I'd like him to finish the season.

One other memorable day during that season, we were not too far from the cape and there was a boat about a mile below us. It was damn rough and we were pulling in our nets a little at a time so we could keep the boat on even keel because of the very rough water. At the same time, we were picking our nets a little at a time because we didn't want the stern too heavy. We were happy because we had half our nets in and would have a nice trim load.

I was keeping an eye out for the other boat, because I noticed that one of the fishermen was pulling his nets into the stern without picking the fish out and his stern was getting a little too heavy for the weather.

I ended up being right. There they were, those two guys, hanging on to the mast and both waving like hell. The stern was completely under and the only thing that saved them was the trapped air in the forecastle. It kept the bow out of the water.

I told Dennis to cut the net loose while I hoisted sail. He must have known exactly where his sharp hatchet was, because he had the net cut loose in a few seconds.

I had to sail away from the other boat in order to get speed to turn around. It took quite a while to do so with a loaded, clumsy sailboat.

When we got to them, they were both yelling.

"We thought you'd sail away! God! We thought you sailed away!"

We decided to take them to their cannery and deliver what fish we had.

On the way there, one guy started bailing water with the handbailer. He was only bailing a cup or less at a time. I told him to stop and have a smoke.

"There's no water in the boat. You're only bailing a spoonful at a time anyway," I said.

The guy replied, "That's all right. That's all right."

I let him keep bailing until he got over his panic. And I'll never forget the other guy. He kept saying, "My bottle of rum. My bottle of rum."

They got over their panic after a bit, and one of

44

them picked the few fish that were in the nets and the other took the tiller.

I didn't see them again, because after we had coffee, I took a nap. Dennis woke me up at our tally station. He said he took them to their cannery and went through all the good-byes and handshakes.

Dennis was always asking stupid questions. Some of the guys told him to keep the "boat hatchet" really sharp and know where it was so he could cut the net loose if we caught a "Bristol Bay Sea Elephant." He also had a piece of sheet-lead and tacks to patch the hull if it was holed by "Bristol Bay Spear Whale."

These were issue items—we had a small hatchet and hammer combo. There was a small piece of sheet-lead issue for emergency patches. His knowing where the hatchet was helped us get to that sinking boat as quick as we did.

One time, we were bucking tide next to the shore and hit a rock or something that made a hole big enough so it wouldn't stay afloat unless we were continuously bailing water. We put it on the beach and patched it with Dennis's big tacks and sheet lead.

Afterwards I told those guys who suggested this hatchet for Sea Elephant business, "You guys were pretty smart to tell Dennis to have his Sea Elephant ax sharp and ready. His having it ready helped us save those guys who were drowning."

I made sure I was far enough away from them—they couldn't get hold of me.

This being Dennis's very first fishing season, he got really sick the first time it got rough. One of his heaves splattered between us and right onto the fish. I ended up getting sick too. After that, I never ate canned salmon for a very long time.

Frank

I had another partner, a "half-breed" like me. He was a fisherman, a mechanic, a trapper, a hi-boat, and a drunk. His name was Frank.

In the spring we had quite a lot of work to do to get the boat ready. Fall time, same thing. Clean it and put everything in the net loft. And I did it all by myself without any help from Frank.

From the first day to the end, every time we had to go back out, I would go get my partner. He would be hung over and he would sleep while I sailed to the fishing grounds. After we got there, he would wake up and send me up the mast.

Getting up the mast was easy because a sailboat is very steady in the water. The sail keeps it from rocking too much. All I had to do was walk up the sail rungs to the saddle between the top of the mast and the sprit. Once up there, I couldn't see the boats most of the time, but I did see their sails.

Then Frank would ask, "What's over east?"

I responded with, "Two sailing out."

He'd say,"How about west?"

My answer: "Lots of them going there."

He said, "Come down."

My partner always seemed to have this instinct for finding fish. But that's not the only reason I fished with him. Another reason I stayed with him was that he was nuts.

Like one time it was dead calm and glassy smooth with billions of fish and no limit. We kept loading and pretty soon I started to insist on delivering.

But all he said was "What the hell's the matter with you? Can't I ever teach you anything? See? The scow is close by and the water? Look at it! Smooth as glass. We could load this thing 'til we have one-inch free board, and by that time it can't sink! Water can't get in if the damn boat is full of fish. Won't have room for water, you dummy!"

So, we rolled up our clothes in the tent, put them on top of the forecastle and loaded our living quarters with fish. We kept putting out little pieces of net and picked about a hundred at a time. Pretty soon we did have about four inches of free board amid ship.

Finally, I asked if we could go to the scow now and my partner answered, "Yeah, what do you think? They're rolling overboard now. Quit asking foolish questions and start rowing."

I didn't get mad because by this time I was feeling some pride in this operation.

We tied up to the tally scow because the fish scow was taking on other boats and we had to wait our turn. The fish scow was always tied snug up against the stem on the tally scow.

The fishermen were allowed meals on the tally scow whenever they had the chance. We were just about done with our hot cakes and bacon when one of the tallymen opened the door and yelled, "Boat sinking!"

Frank and I ran out and . . . shit! There was our boat, sunk as far as it could go. It did stay upright, probably due to the cement ballast in the stem next to the keel for sailing empty.

We found out then that a "monkey boat," a small tow boat, had come past the barges and made enough waves to sink us. They towed us ashore and left us on the beach so we could get the water out when the tide went out. We were beached pretty close to a cannery. So, after the tide went out, I went there and got a five-gallon can for bailing.

I was bailing like hell when my partner showed up. Needless to say, he wasn't too happy to find me bailing.

"Goddamn! What are you doing?"

"Can't you see?" I said. "I'm getting the water out you put in, Boss."

"Stop!"

I did as he asked, then he said. "Now! How long do you think it's going to take to bail four thousand gallons of water? Figure it out, smarty!"

"Well, I can't find the plug! Damn Water is too deep," I replied.

"Okay then," my partner said. "Go to the cannery and get a hose. And don't get a damn garden hose. Get a steam hose."

"Shit! I know what to get! But I don't know anybody."

"Damn, you don't need to know nothing. Just get the hose," he said.

When I took off, he hollered, "Hey, deck hand. Don't let anyone see you."

"Admiral, I'm not that dumb!" I yelled back.

When I got back with the hose, we started the siphon. It would take about two hour, so we decided to go to the cannery to eat and have a drink. We did find something to eat and Frank knew where to find the drinks.

After the two-hour time span was over, I went to check on the boat. I must have put the hose in just the fight place because the boat was dry. I went back and told Frank about the boat and that we should be ready to float in six hours. Frank said he thought he knew something about tides without me telling him. How come he was boss if he didn't know anything about the tides? I, then, proceeded to tell him that if he could find booze in a dry camp he could be boss all he wanted.

He was older than I was, but we were both young enough; so a little drinking didn't hurt us.

The boat was almost afloat when we returned to it. We spent our time looking around. There were five fish, the mast, sail, and a frying pan. We had several lines too. There was the anchor and its spliced-on line. The towline was spliced as well. Then there was the sheet line, or halyard. There was enough offshore wind to put the sail up without the boom and get to the scow. When the boat floated, we waited aboard until the tide ebbed.

We all had "fishermen's slippers." They were

leather shoes that slipped on easily. Just before we "swamped," I bought a brand new pair for four dollars. Now they cost ninety dollars. I still wear them.

On our way out to the scow, I was cleaning one of my slippers.

Frank saw me and said, "Goddamnit! I'm going to fire you! But I need a dummy and I can't find one dumber than you!"

"What the hell is wrong now?" I said.

"How come you're cleaning that shoe? You gonna hop around on one foot?" he asked.

I didn't say anything but I did throw my shoe overboard.

Once we were tied to the barge, a tallyman came running up with a brand new shoe in hand.

"I found one of your shoes. It was hung up on the scow."

Frank took one look at me and took off. I chased him around the barge twice before I gave up. I realized later that I'd be the one overboard because Frank was bigger than I was.

We were among the higher average boats. Not because we worked harder, but because Frank knew how to cheat.

When the flat-scows got full, they just untied them from the tally scow and anchored them out to wait for the tide.

Even if the sun didn't go down for long, it got pretty damn dark on rainy nights. Shit, we'd just go and get our fish from one of anchored scows. We only did this once.

At other times, when there was lots of fish, we just cut the fish out of the net instead of working the web loose. It was about twice as fast and the holes didn't hurt the fish catch when there was a lot of fish. When the fish slacked off, we just got another net. We got it one way or another. If there were rotten spots in it, we would just cut it loose and say we lost it. It was all company gear.

When we were "over limit," the extra fish were given to other fishermen who had come in short. It was almost always left to the tallyman to decide who got the fish. We always gave the tallyman booze.

When we would go ashore once a week, which was usually Sunday, we had lots of help. There always were guys who would help us blue stone our nets, grub up, and watch our boat. They did this for a pint of whiskey, which had more value than money.

Frank was always doing something.

One time he came running to me, wanting me to help patch his roof. I said I would once the rain quit. He responded with, "No use to fix the damn thing when it's not raining! Because, you damn fool, it doesn't leak when it's not raining."

Another time, he wanted me to help him take grub to his trapping cabin. He had some kind of three-wheel motorbike. We borrowed a wooden sled to haul the stuff. There were three of us who went: Frank, a Greek, and I. Well, Frank and I were on the bike while the Greek rode on the sled.

Well, the river was frozen smooth as glass. There was no snow, just ice. Frank got the three-wheeler going on the ice and couldn't slack off the throttle. He got the bike going as fast as it would go, the sled started swinging back and forth on the ice. The Greek was hanging on for whatever he figured life was worth.

Then the sled hit a crack in the ice. There were pieces of sled, rice, flour, traps, and everything else imaginable scattered across the ice for a quarter of a mile because it took Frank that long before he glanced back. Even the Greek was sprawled on the ice.

We salvaged one bottle of booze. The Greek and I went back to town to replace the sled. I don't know what happened after that because we never went back.

Frank had a twelve-volt Windmill for lights. He started picking up old batteries. He must have had every old battery in the village. The mess was twisted together with a spider web of old wire. One windy day this thing blew up. He wanted me to help clean up the mess. There were busted windows, broken glass, pieces of battery and acid everywhere. I refused to join that project.

We used to have riverboats, or skiffs as we called them. They were about twenty-two feet long. They were real narrow on the bottom, and fat on the top, with a narrow stem. A ten-horse Johnson outboard propelled the skiff. This was when Johnson first came out with a ten-horse. It had two cylinders, and not much else, besides a flywheel. I wish I had one now.

Frank had borrowed one of these riverboats, and he wanted me to go with him and his partner to his winter trapping cabin. I was to bring the boat back to the owner. He also brought three dogs and dog food.

The dog food was dried salmon in one hundred-pound bundles. The salmon were mostly seven pounders with their heads cut off. The only reason for cutting the head off was that salmon have surprisingly large sharp teeth, and the gills don't dry out so good. We split the salmon down the backbone and belly, leaving the guts inside.

We'd hung the fish on a rack made from two beams and several three-inch poles placed between them. The whole fish was dried. Slime, blood, guts, everything. They even got moldy. This was probably why the dogs never got sick. Talk about "one-a-day" pills with iron!

In that damn boat, we had fish, flour, sugar, and canned goods. We, also, carried lots of yeast hops, sugar, and dried fruit for beer making.

We were going about two hundred miles up river, at thirty miles a day. It didn't take much gas because the machine didn't use too much and they knew how to follow the eddies. I already figured out I was to row back.

We tied the boat along the shore and camped there at night, or if it was a good place to get a beaver or a duck to eat. I think the dogs were satisfied; they ate the same food we did. The dried dog food was their winter emergency rations.

The boat sprang a bad leak and Frank had fixed up a plunger pump, with a hose leading to the bottom. The thing worked pretty well for the first fifty miles.

One morning, Frank came to me.

"You pump the boat last night?"

"Yeah, sure. Why?" I asked.

"Come take a look," he replied.

What a mess! Try emptying a sunken boat full to the gunwale with slimy dogfish, wet flour sacks, canned food that broke apart, and hops. There were shotgun shell cases, traps, wine, rope, tarps, and winter clothes. All of it was mixed in with gas and oil.

We cleaned the boat, just splashed a little water on the deck so it wouldn't be slippery. Then we headed back to Dillingham.

We salvaged the rifles, shotguns, all the hardware, and the dogs. We'd found only one oar and had to make another one before we headed back down river. There were three of us rowing the fifty miles instead of just me rowing by myself. Needless to say, Frank lost that trapping season.

At the time, the homes we lived in had one or two rooms with two doors leading out. Going out one door led to a very small room and the outer door. We called this room the windbreak. We stored dog harnesses, shovels, and everything else we could in this room.

Well, Frank and I woke up one morning in the windbreak. It was very cold. I remember Frank giving me some advice I'll never forget.

He said, "Don't ever get married again."

Bill

Bill helped me rebuild an old boat. This thing was a sail boat converted from sail to power. The old gasoline engine was pretty much gone and I bought an engine (almost as bad as the one in it) to replace it. He helped me repair the engine and install it. When the engine was installed, I told him we would fish it together that season and asked him to make the living quarters a little more livable—while I took care of a lot of important business.

It was a week or ten days before I went back to see how things were going—my "important business" was done anyway.

I expected him to have some kind of damn shelter for us—I sure got a surprise. He had the over-the-forecastle cabin done. With a small cast-iron heater-cook stove. The cabin had two bunks and small windows. He said he was going to paint it that evening.

I said, "Let's go to the mess hall and get us a cup of coffee"—this was at Alaska Packers Clark's Point Cannery—Nushagak. During coffee I told him, "We can always paint the thing later—let's try it on the water." He thought it probably would be a good idea to try it.

On the way out of the coffee room I said, "We'll get out nets and other fishing gear and see how they fit."

We wound up with a conversion that was I thought—better than the conversions the canneries had—because it had a wood cabin instead of a piece of sheet iron.

We parked it too near the beach in Dillingham and a flood wrecked it that fall.

That winter I bought a fiberglass "inflate" and shipped it to Dillingham. Bill and I fished it with Danny.

Once we were having a bite to eat with incoming tide. When I told the guys to tell Bill to come and eat.

"He's too sick to eat—he hasn't eaten for two days now."

"Why didn't you tell me? We may have to take him to the hospital."

"He said that's what you'd do and he doesn't want to stop you from fishing."

I went to his bunk and asked him. I asked him and he said "There's something real bad wrong with my stomach. I can't get out of bed."

There was no fish and we only had fifty fathoms out to hold us in the channel.

The *Belle II* was new and from below the Ekuk light to Dillingham harbor took us just a few minutes more than one hour.

The ambulance was waiting and took him to Kanakanak Hospital, and they shipped him right to Anchorage. I was told they removed those gallstones just in time.

Bill was different from any of my fishing partners or crew— he didn't drink.

I fished sail for twelve years, and had five different partners.

Flying

Aeroncia C-3

My first plane was an Aeroncia C-3. It was, I believe, one of the first personal use aircraft built in America—after the Wright brothers.

It was a two-place tandem with a wooden prop connected to a two-cylinder, air-cooled engine. I believe it put out thirty-three horsepower, but the horses were half-dead.

The fuselage and wings were pieces of metal and wood all wrapped in some damn good cloth.

This thing didn't have wing struts like the small aircraft we see today; it had guide wires.

There was a metal post about two feet long connected to the top of the fuselage and a wire ran to somewhere past the center of the wing on the main spar. The bottom of the wing had two flat rods. These rods were made of flat steel about 1/8 x 3/4 inches. They were connected to both spars.

When it was in the air, those damn rods would vibrate—one would have a laying down "8" and the other a "2" edged knifelike shape or a stretched out "O." What unnerved me was they didn't keep the same shape. The one that made an "8" would trade it to the other one for its stretched "O."

I only made three trips in this thing. Because of this and because I would have to clean the plugs every time I wanted to start the engine. Plus, I could never get the thing off the ground with a passenger.

One day I caught Red at the lake—our winter landing area. After a lot of begging, Red finally said OK.

He got the thing in the air with the two of us. He made a long, careful turnaround and landed. Without a word, he got out of it and walked off. I tried to call him back, but he didn't look back or slow his fast pace. He walked straight back to town. I came to the conclusion that he didn't like me or my plane.

The next day, I took it to my garage and started to work. I took a hacksaw and cut the wings off, then I chopped off part of the fuselage ahead of the tail rudder and elevator group.

I wound up with a snow machine.

As I remember, I went smelting a lot of times. The smelt hole were about five miles from the village where I lived. Since this distance was over ice and snow, my wingless bird was the perfect vehicle for the trip.

I found I had a lot of friends that I didn't know I had previously. They were generous friends too! They bought gas for the machine and always presented me with a bottle.

One day, a local bar owner asked me to take him to a place that he was told had land-locked salmon—he caught two. On the way home, he offered me five hundred bucks and one hundred dollars for my snow machine, just to make conversation and not show too much panic. I said, "Plus how bottles?" The bar owner said, "And five bottles, good many whiskey!"

He must have forgotten to bring his spare spark plugs on one of his trips, because he sold it to a couple of native guys. These guys lived in a village a short distance from Dillingham. They used it for a couple of winters, back and forth to Dillingham.

Some time later, a guy came and asked me about my airplane. He said he represented a museum. When I told him what happened to it, he just shook his head and walked off. I recently found out that the only Aeronica C-3 left in one piece is in a museum.

I guess I knew all the time because as I was working on the damn thing and a guy comes up to me and says, "Working on that museum piece again, Walt?"

How I got the plane in the first place? A friend of mine, Stan, came to me in Dillingham saying he needed a hundred bucks to get back to Anchorage.

It was my turn to borrow from him, so I said, "Shit, no, I don't."

He said, "I'll give you my Aeroncia C-3."

"What is that?" I asked.

"It's a two-place airplane I bought in Anchorage and it quit on me across the Wood River from here," he replied.

Me: "That country is mostly swamp. How much damage when it flipped over?"

Stan: "It didn't turn over. I happened to find a good spot and by that big slough too."

Stan went on to say that he paid three hundred for

it, and I'd owe him one hundred more if I took the plane.

I agreed and gave him the money.

(I've been pretty drunk since then, but I never got that feeling to pay that hundred bucks to Stan, because it cost eight quarts to get it out.)

The next day I went downtown, thinking I might find somebody a little thirsty. Sure enough, down on the waterfront were four guys sitting on their skiffs and sipping their last bottle. Each of them had an eighteen-foot skiff with an outboard motor.

I approached them. "Hi! You guys want to work a little bit and get two quarts apiece?"

"Sure we work," the leader said.

Everything went just right. The tide was just right, on the flood. The weather was calm. And we got to where the plane was on time.

Before they left for their walk to the plane, I told them, "Now I want to tell you the best way to move that thing."

I explained that one guy was to be at the narrow part, that the end was light and easy to lift. He would be the leader. The rest of them were to get hold of the thing and push.

When they got back to the skiffs, I had the skiffs tied together and had the planks in place to roll the plane aboard.

After we got the plane aboard, tied down, and ready to head for Dillingham, I commented, "Damn! You got that thing here in a hurry!"

"Yeah, we don't stop and rest like you say. We

have to hurry before liquor store close and we got nothing but water 'til morning," they replied.

Again, the tide was with us and we made it to Dillingham in no time.

We loaded the plane onto my flatbed Chevy and took it to my yard. I drove them to the liquor store. I wasn't cheap. I bought full quarts, only the whiskey was cheap.

One of them had the foresight to ask me to take them to the beach where I found them. He knew if they tried to carry that stuff through town, they'd never make it to their boats with their day's pay.

J-5 Gold

Two young guys came to me wanting to check a creek that was full of gold. We took off the next morning. Our landing at the mouth of the creek was at tidewater.

When we landed there was a good twenty-mile-per-hour wind. I noticed the gravel had no binder and therefore the landing wheels sunk into the gravel, making it stop pretty quick. I told the guys that we might have a problem at take-off if the wind died down. They said they'd hurry.

The damn wind did drop down to almost nothing. They insisted we try for take-off. The plane didn't budge. The only thing that I could think of was for the guys to push the plane to get it started. I told them that I'd get a charter on floats. They didn't like this at all.

During this exchange of ideas, one of them said, "The only reason we asked you was that you were the only one who would take us for nothing!"

Finally one of them came up with an idea I felt might work.

"You said that if we push you could take off?"

"Yes," I said.

"We'll push and hop in when you tell us," he said.

"Okay. But I'll have to take the door off."

The door was on pin hinges and easily removed.

That's when the crazy and goofy part started. We decided they would push until the plane got moving, then they would climb aboard.

When the plane got going good, I hollered for them to get aboard. The first guy got in, but the other guy was still outside.

This is what I heard behind me:

"Hang onto me!"

"I'm hanging on!"

"Pull harder!"

"Tell him not to go over the water. I can't swim!"

"I hear you. I'm over the water, so you don't land on the rocks!"

I thought he would be better off drowned than to have his head dashed on the rocks.

He finally got aboard. I headed for a spot not too far away to put the door back on. There was no noise behind me, so I looked back. Both of my passengers had their face and head covered with their coats.

The windblast from the open door didn't affect

me, but in the back seat, there was a very cold, strong draft.

They didn't say a damn thing until we were putting the door back on. One of them was still sore about flying over the water. I shut them up when I said, "I'll leave you here if you don't shut up." They were quiet until we got to Dillingham.

After we got the plane tied down at the airstrip in Dillingham, one of them asked, "We could have a drink in your house?"

My wife was getting tired of those "after prospecting parties, "so I told them I'd buy them one at the bar. That's when I made my second mistake. The story of our trip was retold to everyone at the bar!

My first mistake was taking them prospecting. My third mistake was taking them prospecting in the first place!

The Rescue

This J-5 was used in a short flight rescue.

A local man named John came to me one day and told me there was a guy across the mouth of Wood River—"waving his arms like hell!"

It was towards spring and Wood River already had open water, and he couldn't get across. There was still good ice on the land.

I decided to pick the guy up and John went along with me. There was a very strong wind and I landed within a few feet of the guy with no noticeable ground speed. The wind velocity was the same as my landing speed.

In Dillingham, we took the guy to the restaurant so he could warm up and eat.

This trip was especially memorable because of what John said to me as I drove him home.

He said, "Walt, you landed standing still. Why don't you land like that all the time?"

Wolverine

I was in this J-5, on skies, when I had to land for the weather. I landed on a lake. I knew the weather was clearing ahead of me, and clearing fast, so I didn't have long to wait to avoid a "turn around."

I wasn't there very long before a wolverine started to cross the lake. I let him get halfway across when I started my engine. I had to warm it up anyway and I started chasing the wolverine.

He, evidently, got tired of this foolishness. He let me get close, then turned around and took a swipe at the plane. It scared the "p" out of me because he did the swiping on my side of the plane. His claws looked pretty damn big through my side window.

Then he started chasing *me*! He chased me halfway around that lake. Then he stopped for a few seconds, then nonchalantly started to walk off. I let him go, not wanting to continue my wolverine chase.

I thought to myself. *Noden boy, you probably have better things to do besides chasing a stupid wolverine.*

64

I had another encounter with a wolverine. It happened when another guy and I caught a moose.

We couldn't take all the meat that evening, but we took as much as we could. We planned to return early the following morning for the rest of it.

We arrived to where we had the meat that morning and found evidence that a wolverine had helped himself to some of our moose. He had eaten part of it and urinated on the remainder. Wolverines will urinate on meat that they want to keep for themselves. I don't believe there is another animal that will eat meat that a wolverine has urinated on, except maybe another wolverine.

I hated and respected him at the same time, because he was a fighter. The big, old Alaska bear has respect for him too, and probably for the same reason.

The Trade

I traded this J-5 to a guy for a small, fifty-foot power barge called the *Wood River Belle*. Albert was visiting me, and I noticed he kept looking at his watch. I'd never seen him do that before.

"You've been looking at your watch more than once. You going someplace?" I asked.

"No, I'm selling the *Belle*. I'm meeting the guy downtown; he's giving me a thousand for it tonight," Albert replied.

"Hell! I'll give you that plus my J-5, to boot!" I said.

"Wait! Wait! Wait! Let me use your phone!" Albert said.

He used the phone and after awhile, he returned with his hand out. "Okay, Walt, shake! I get the cash and your J-5, and you get the Belle."

"Okay, Albert, shake!" And we shook hands.

Then Albert announced, "I'm afraid I can't help you finish up the bear I brought. Gusty and I are going for a plane ride!"

The *Wood River Belle* was the first power scow in Bristol Bay, I believe. The Columbia Ward Packing Company had built her as an experiment m hauling fish, using self-propelled barges.

They had a salmon cannery on the Wood River, located just a little above Dillingham. The *Belle* never hauled one fish to that cannery. It ran aground on its first run with a load, which happened at the highest tide of the season. The cannery salvaged it, hauling it up on their ways, where it sat until Albert bought it. It was pretty much useless for him because by that time, bigger, more powerful twin-screw barges were in use.

But the *Belle* was good to me. I used it on small hauling jobs, like the contract I got to haul raw fish to a small cannery. My crew consisted of mostly my family.

Harvey

Harvey came to me and told me that Bill was long overdue. He hadn't returned from a trip to the upper Mulchatna in his two-place Taylercraft. It was towards spring, but the weather was still cold enough that we didn't want to have anyone "overdue" too long without having a look. So, we went on a "take a look."

The wind, from the north, got stronger and very rough the farther we went. That damn old J-5 we were in wasn't making much headway. It was bouncing up and down and sideways just as much as moving ahead.

The roughest part of the trip came up and Harvey decided he needed to urinate. He asked me if I had a can or something like that to use.

"No! You'll just have to hold it. I can't land this thing in this weather," I said. "Besides, they'll be looking for us too if I did."

I told him to open the door a crack and do his business. After some words about me and my plane, he replied, "Dammit, I can't. You'll just have to land!"

"There's a piece of four-inch stove pipe back there that I use with my engine heater. Try that," I said.

Soon I heard more cussing from behind me. I looked back to see what the problem was. There was Harvey. He had one foot holding the plane door open a crack. The other foot was under my seat. One hand gripped the top of the pilot's seat while the other hand was trying to connect the pipe to himself.

"Dammit! Just go on the floor, but you'll be cleaning it up when we get into town!" I replied.

Needless to say we found Billy. When we flew over the cabin where Billy was, we saw that his plane was tied down and that everyone was standing at the lee of the cabin. When I started my turn for home, they gave us a hello-good-bye wave. We made it home in pretty good timing because of the good tail wind.

The next day I found Harvey.

"I'll drive you to my plane so you can clean up your mess," I said.

"Noden, I urinate in planes. I don't clean up stupid guy's planes that have been pissed in." Harvey replied.

Super Cub: Babies

I was in a ski-equipped Piper Super Cub, on my way to Dillingham. I landed at one of the villages that were located on the Nushagak River just to see if anyone wanted to go with me to Dillingham.

Sure enough! A guy came running up to me and asked if I could wait for a woman who needed to get to the hospital there.

When she arrived at the plane, I noticed that she was real big.

"Baby?" I asked.

"Yes, baby," she answered.

Within a few moments of our arrival in Dillingham, she began to say "Hurry up! Hurry up!"

Just before landing she was half crying and saying the same thing.

I landed as close to the hospital as I could, taxied through the brush trying to get as close to the door as possible. I got out and ran to tell the hospital people that I had a stretcher case. I, also, mentioned that it was a "hurry up" sort of thing.

I followed the stretcher out to the plane to help, then back to the hospital.

I was pretty shook up thinking about what I could or couldn't have done if she had had that baby in my plane. I decided to rest a bit at the hospital before heading out. After my nerves were calm, I walked out to my plane. I heard someone yelling at me, so I turned to see what the person wanted. A nurse was outside waving her arms and yelling, "Wait! Wait! Come back! Come back! You had triplets! You had triplets!"

We were in an airplane with "sitting room only" for two and there were two of us. We were in the air and we were flying. She was going to have one baby, not three!

As I write this, years later, I still get the same feelings I had then. I left the plane where it was and took a cab home. I decided that I was just a bit too shaky to fly.

Billy

Billy was a young man just starting out in life. And like all men, he was making a home. He was building a cabin in the lower Tickchik Lake area, about seventy air miles from Dillingham.

Billy was reported missing on a trip to his cabin in an old snow traveler. It consisted of a piece of rubber conveyer belting with angle iron cleats connected to a small gas engine.

This was about 1960 and "snow machines" were just coming into use and were not very reliable.

Word got out that he was missing and his friends (mostly the younger generation) started a search by dog team. I believe there were two teams involved. The Air Taxi pilots would "take a look" when they had a chance and the fuel to spare.

Two days had passed before a dog team reported finding Billy's snow traveler in a wood patch that was located in a large crusted snow-covered flat.

The ones who finished the search arrived by dog team to the sight. They were equipped with snowshoes and skis.

They found three snow shoe marks in the crusted snow. The search team looked for more, but nothing else turned up on that wind-blown hard snow-covered flat.

They didn't give up. They kept trying. Now, they decided that if they could get a trained dog, they had a chance. The search team found Shorty and "Dog." They lived in the Palmer, Anchorage area. Contact was made and Shorty agreed to bring "Dog," his tracker, to Dillingham.

When Shorty and "Dog" arrived via Peterson's Northern Consolidated Airlines, I took them both to the search area. One of the dog teams was there.

Shorty brought Dog to the snow shoe marks. He let her smell one of Billy's caps, then said, "Go find." She went back and forth through those three tracks about eight feet each way.

Dog was bleeding so badly that I got a little nervous.

"She's going to bleed to death. You should take her off of it," I told Shorty.

"I can't, Walt. She'll be hurt if I took her off now. She'll be so hurt that she might never work again."

"What the hell is she doing?" I asked.

Shorty looked and said, "She's finding which direction Billy went in. The scent gets stronger in the direction he's going."

About this time Dog looked back at Shorty, gave a woof, and took off. She had her nose close to the snow, but wasn't touching it.

"Walt, we'll find him now! I've got to follow her. You take off once in awhile and I'll wave you down when we find him," Shorty replied.

The dog team followed Shorty and Dog. I took off every hour or close to it. It must have been about my third takeoff when I saw Shorty and Dog coming back.

He told me that they had found him covered with drift snow behind a small, lone tree where he tried to take shelter.

I brought Dog and Shorty back to Dillingham before dark that day. The search organizers had a going-away party for them a few days later at Paul's house where they changed Dog's name to Queenie.

Tom

Tom Overvik was a sailor in Alaska who fished, trapped, and lived alone. I met Tom in Libby's Ekuk during my first fishing season. I fished with Roy Furrie at the time. We stayed at the same bunkhouse. (It was an unused fish tally station barge-on its way to retirement.) This one was laid up on the scow ways. I didn't have much to do with him at this time because I didn't spend much time at the bunk scow. I hung around people my own age during my leisure time. He was always friendly to me and I liked him.

The last time I saw Tom was in his small log cabin on the Malchatna River.

The commissioner (this was a person appointed by government to take care of legal work for each designated area, such as our area Bristol Bay) sent word that he wanted to see me. I went and Dave said, "Walt, you know Tom died."

"No, I didn't. When did he die?" I said.

"I don't know. Bill told me he went to go visit him and found him dead in his cabin," Dave said. "Everyone I've talked to doesn't want to give a dead guy a ride on credit. There's no allotted money for his ride to Dillingham. If you would pick him up, the Fish and Game will follow in their plane as a legal party for the cabin inspection. They will help all they can. The only thing is they can't take Tom in their plane. If you'll do this, I'll do all I can to get you paid from his estate. What do you say Walt?"

"Dave," I said, "I'd rather have Tom owe me dead than half the guys alive who owe me now. But do you think you could find someone to ride with me? I may be a little too nervous to ride alone with him."

Mike volunteered to go with me. He'd been in the office when we were talking.

Mike and I took my plane and the Fish and Game guys followed in a government plane.

We arrived at the cabin before the others. Mike and I stood outside the cabin door for a while, but ended up going inside due to the cold wind.

It was a small cabin. At the right of the door was a small cast-iron stove. Against the far wall was a wooden bunk. Tom was in it. He was stark naked and frozen stiff. At the head of the bed was a wooden coal oil box that held two five-gallon cans, either of gas or kerosene. On top of this box was a book. On top of the book was a full quart of unopened rum.

I went and picked up the book and opened it to the last page and realized it was Tom's diary. I began to read.

Today I burned my last stick of wood.

Day two: I burned the chair today.

Day three: Managed to put the last piece of meat on the floor for the cat, although I don't believe that house cats are human eaters.

Day four: The wolves are howling closer every day. They must know I'm on my last sail. . . .

There were no more entries after this.

Before each day's entry, he had the date and weather condition.

The two wardens came in and read the diary. As they made their check of the cabin, I snitched the bottle. I know they had to have noticed that it was gone. I had hidden it under my heavy coat, but no one said a thing.

Our next problem concerned the cat. We tried

thinking of people in Dillingham who would take the thing. No name came up. Who in their right mind would want to own a dead man's cat? We ended up drawing straws to see who got to put the poor beast out of its misery. Okay! The cat didn't suffer. He was shot in the head with a high-powered pistol.

Again we pulled straws. This time to see who had to bury the cat. The loser walked behind the cabin with the cat. Another followed to see that the cat was given a decent burial through four feet of snow and three feet of frozen ground. The burial party returned too quickly to have gotten the cat past a good snow burial.

The planes were parked in different places, so the game wardens went to their plane. Mike and I tried to carry Tom to my plane.

He wasn't a big man, just skin and bone frozen straight and stiff as a board. The snow was real deep, so when one of us went through the snow crust, the other would fall down along with Tom.

Finally Mike said, "Walt, let's just one of us carry Tom. You go to the plane and get it ready—I'll be pretty close behind. And at least I won't have you dragging Tom and me into the snow every other step."

So Mike ended up carrying Tom by himself, while I went and started the plane. By the time Mike arrived, the plane was warmed up and ready to go.

When we got to Dillingham, we tied the plane down for the night. I drove Mike home and went to tell Dave that Tom would stay in my plane for the night since there was no place to keep him this late. He asked if I thought it was all right. I told him it was and that I thought Tom wouldn't mind. Besides, who's gonna bother a plane with a dead guy in it?

Tom's bottle of rum followed me home from the plane that night. On the way home from Tom's cabin, I had the time to plan the rum's demise. As soon as I stepped in the door, I told my wife Florence to go find Paul and his wife while I changed out of my winter flying clothes.

That evening we had a "Good-bye, Tom" party.

In those days everybody used the porcelain coffee mugs from the salmon cannery. We were no different.

The next morning I cleared the table while Florence made breakfast. As I did this, I noticed that there were *five* used mugs instead of just four. I asked Florence who else had been there. She told me that it had just been the four of us. I asked Paul about it and his answer was the same.

We went over the incident again and again. We kept getting the same answer. It had only been the four of us. So, where did the fifth mug come from? There was only one explanation. Tom had a drink with us that night.

Dave let me know that if he could find no family of Tom's to pay for the charter, he was going to sign Tom's cabin over to me. That meant I'd have to make a bill for the trip and I just didn't have the heart to do it. Tom was a man who loved my mother's country and I didn't want to charge for his last ride on earth.

When you come right down to answering questions, when Tom and I meet again, I can tell him that I was paid in full. The untouched rum was my charge.

The Moose

The local aircraft mechanic came to me and asked me if I would do a little work for him. I told him that I would be happy and proud to be able to do something—but what?

"Tom wants to go moose hunting for winter meat for his family. He's been asking me every day for sometime now. I can't do the work unless I license that plane and I won't do it. If you just do a little welding for him, he can get his moose. If you'll just show him how to prepare for the welds and weld for him, we can forget about the whole thing." I said okay.

Ken was a licensed aircraft mechanic. Tom didn't have the money to rebuild the thing and Ken was too busy working "pay" jobs.

Tom and I went through the preparation procedure. He did the work and I welded it. Tom went moose hunting.

The next thing I know, another pilot came to see me and asked if I could help him ferry a moose that Tom had shot. Tom could not move it out because he got the moose on a sand bar that was too short to get the plane off with any part of the moose.

I told Dick okay. In those days pilots used to help each other out when they could. There wasn't anyone else to look out for each other but other pilots.

We decided that we were going to follow Tom out to where the moose was. A friend of mine, "Fenning," was listening to all our plans and came to me with his part of the plan.

I took him with me and dropped him and his gear at a good spot and was to him up the next day with his moose.

Tom was in the lead, next came Dick, then it was Fenning and I bringing up the rear. When Tom circled the place where his moose was, I recognize it as the spot I'd looked at two days before. Dick had told me there was a moose in the area.

I didn't go back because I could never get any meat off the short sandbar. All three of us landed on a larger bar. Dick and I brought all the meat to Tom's plane. It took awhile because we were only able to carry a little at a time, but we did get it all. After that we headed for home.

It was late and pitch black by the time we arrived in Dillingham. None of the planes involved had navigation lights. The batteries were removed to lighten the planes.

I kept my plane at the east end of what we called the "short field" and Tom had a house along the side of the strip. There was water along the south side of the strip. Tom's house was on the west end.

Anyway, I was landing, using the shiny water as a guide. Tom was landing in the opposite direction at the same time, using his house light for a guide. Neither of us knew that the other plane was anywhere near the other. The two planes had collided somewhere near the middle of the landing strip.

It must have been only seconds before I woke up to hear Feening yelling, "Help, help, my balls are busted. My balls are busted."

Apparently Feening's seatbelt had broken and he had hit the rear pilot control with his manly parts.

I smelled gas, so it didn't take me long to get Feening out. He kept saying not to move him fast because of his busted parts. I turned and saw that the airplanes were side by side, with the engines next to each other.

I ran to Tom's side and opened his door. I remember telling him to get out because the planes might blow up. He responded with "I can't, my head is busted." I had to drag him out too.

People got there pretty quick and we hopped into a cab that was there. The cabdriver took the three of us to the A.N.S. hospital in Kanakanak.

Once there, the nurse seated us and ran for the doctor. It wasn't too long before he joined us.

"Mr. Noden, I'd like to take the worst case first," the doc said.

"Well, Doc, this guy beside me has busted balls and the other one has a broken head. So, take your pick. I'm all right. I'm just sore all over," I replied.

In a louder voice, he said, "Mr. Noden, I'll take the testes case first."

"Greek, that's you. Go! You're the testes," I said.

Feening was led away. Then the nurse took Tom away. Two minutes later she came up to me and said, "Have you seen his hair?"

I didn't know what she was talking about. "What hair?"

"Never mind. What car did you come in?" she asked.

"The cab outside. I told him to wait," I said.

She went out and came back in with something cupped in her hands.

"What's going on?" I asked.

She gave me a small giggle as her answer. And kept on going.

I found out later that Tom had lost a piece his scalp. He had something like an extra compass somewhere in the area that his head hit on impact, scalping him. The scalp was sewn back on, but it left a small bald spot as a memento.

After that we told the "Greek" that he was a man with nothing but testes, but no balls at all.

On my way home, I was thinking that I possibly couldn't have any more problems. I was wrong.

As soon as I walked in the door, I greeted my wife with "How's things been with you today?"

My wife replied, "You promised! You promised to come home to vote with me!"

It happened to be Election Day and I had sworn to go vote with her.

"Tom was looking for you this morning. I told him I'd send you right over. You'd better hurry up and go see him," My wife said.

All I could say was "Honey, I found Tom!"

Our planes were total wrecks and were never repaired.

That was the end of my Piper Super Cub.

Now, as I write I still get shaking mad about it because it was all my fault!

I helped get Tom's plane in the air. I helped get the meat from a strip of land I wouldn't land on to get my *own* meat. I was flying without lights because we took the batteries out because of the weight problem.

Word of the wreck got out of the Dillingham area and one of the members of the *Airplane Owners and Pilots Association* mentioned the fact that, "even bicycles have lights."

Aeronca Sedan

I used an Aeronca Sedan for a lot of my flying. The thing was slower than a mule train, but it was a four-place and could carry a good load of freight.

I bought the thing in Pendleton, Oregon. A friend of mine in Seattle said that he'd drive me to Pendleton and I'd fly him to Dillingham, Alaska.

In Pendelton, we found the seller. We looked the plane over and did the paperwork. By the time all this was done, it was too late to head for Seattle, so we stayed overnight.

Early the next morning, I gave my friend a two-hour lead, then I started for Seattle myself.

Looking at the map, after I was airborne, I decided to follow the Columbia River to Vancouver, then follow the highway to Seattle.

When I got to the river, I lowered my altitude to observe the scenery below. I was being a tourist!

The weather was beautiful and I kind of let the plane fly itself while I took in the scenery. All of a sudden, this damn bridge came charging at me. I opened the throttle all the way and barely made it over the top of the bridge.

I had been flying just over the water because where I was used to flying, in Bristol Bay Alaska, the rivers didn't have any bridges. Only the creeks were bridged.

I told a small group of friends about this. One of them remarked, "Noden, I know what the paper would say . . . 'Alaska Native Battles Bridge—Bridge Wins!' "

I followed the Columbia River until I got to the Portland-Vancouver area. I, then, followed the highway to Seattle.

When I called the Seattle Tower, they were really helpful. Billy had just called, telling them to expect a call from an Alaska Native.

First, the Seattle Tower told me how to get within their vision. When they had me sighted, they gave me altitude and direction. It was right to my tie-down spot where Billy was waiting.

We visited in Seattle for a couple of days. I didn't know that the day I picked to leave for home was a Canadian holiday. It was the Queen of England's birthday.

When we arrived at the airport in Canada, I called in for landing instructions. The tower called back.

"Pip-pip, old man. There's no one working except me. Land any runway. There's no wind."

I, then, asked what runway would be good for gas-up.

"Pip-pip, old man. Land runway nine. Halfway down the runway is gas and oil. There's no one there, but there are no locks. Take whatever you want; it's on the queen. Pip-pip, old man."

We got our gas. Asked for take off. Said our thank-yous and pip-pips. We headed for Anchorage, our "designated point of entry" from a foreign country.

Just before we left Canada, I'd notice a small landing strip on the Canadian side. The weather didn't look good ahead of us and I was looking for a place to land. It wasn't long before we made a turn around and landed at that airstrip. Before landing I circled the strip to try calling attention. After a while, we landed, tied the plane down, and began walking.

We had not walked very long when we came across a bunkhouse- type building. We knocked on the door. There was no answer, so I opened it up. It was a bunkhouse with an aisle and rooms on each side.

We needed to rest and upon finding an empty room, we laid down for a nap.

I was shaken awake by Billy, saying that he smelled smoke. He went to investigate when I heard him say "Come here! It's here!"

I ran to where Billy was and saw this guy lying on the bunk with the mattress on fire. It was mostly smoke, but small flames were beginning to show.

We tried to wake him up by shaking him, but no luck. Billy went so far as to grab the guy's hair to shake him awake. We finally rolled him on the floor, threw the mattress outside, and broke some windows open.

The storm was a small one because it had already cleared when we looked. We took off for Anchorage to "clear customs" and fuel up. The rest of our trip was on a calm, clear day. After landing in Dillingham, Billy said, "Noden, thank you for making one flight without something stupid happening?"

Now, when I think about what Billy said, I think who was involved. There were three people. One was going home from school several thousand miles away. The other flying home an airplane he could use to support his wife and young children. The other, the Queen of England. The Queen bought them the fuel for the trip home. They repaid her by saving one of her subjects. There may have been more fire or smoke caused casualties if someone, other than the passed out Queen's people, hadn't been there just at the right moment.

Helen Faints

There is another memorable incidence with this plane.

I was on a short trip from Dillingham to Ekuk, about twenty miles, with this lady passenger. About halfway to my destination, my engine quit on me. I happened to be close to a gravel beach and made a "dead stick" landing.

"Why did we land here?" my passenger asked.

"My engine quit. I have to get out and see what happened," I informed her.

As soon as I got out of the plane, I saw what happened. One of the cylinder and piston assemblies had broken loose from the engine and was hanging on by the piston and connecting rod assembly.

This model of Continental 145 had a "weak spot" that was rectified in later models.

"You may as well come on out. We aren't going any farther in this plane," I told her.

"What happened, Walt?" she asked.

"Take a look at the engine!"

I have never seen a woman faint before. Now I know how they do it. They make an "Eeeeeeee" sound and their legs get wobbly. Lucky for her I was able to catch her before she hit the gravel. We both ended up sitting on the beach.

I needed to calm down because I had to think of a way to get the plane over some piling stubs sticking out of the beach gravel. I knew that there were a couple of family homes there at Nushagak Point where we landed. This was the site of a Russian fort.

Back when the Russians owned Alaska, Nushigak was the main Russian fort for the Bristol Bay area. Russian artifacts such as cannonballs and other old items can still be found there.

When Alaska became a territory of the United States, one of the larger U.S. salmon processors had a salmon salting station there.

The folks there helped me get my plane off the beach. We had quite a time getting that old "Airknocker" up the beach and past the high-water mark. A rope was tied to the tail end of the plane and with every man, woman, and child pulling together, we got it to a safe spot.

As friendly as they were, they were liars. While we were having a bite to eat, one of them said that he was going to Dillingham in his skiff and we could go with him if we wanted to!

He just did not want to embarrass me by having to ask him for a ride to Dillingham. On our arrival at Dillingham, I gave him enough gas and oil to last for a few trips to Dillingham, also enough bear to last him a few days. This was the Alaskan Native way. A favor for a favor. There were no American dollars involved.

White Fish

I was flying home with a four-place Aeronica float-plane. At the drainage end of a large lake, I saw three large skiffs. I landed and found four guys fishing for white fish for their village's winter supply. The fish were on their spawning migration and were concentrated in that area.

I decided to ask to take some home. They loaded in about a hundred pounds. These fish were pretty large, weighing about two pounds each.

I get to Dillingham and who should I run into? It was a representative for an airline that was making regular trips, might have been twice a week, to Dillingham. I gave him some of the white fish and seeing how large they were, he told me that there might be a sale for them in Anchorage.

I went back to the lake to pick up a planeload, about five hundred pounds. When I got to the guys at the lake, they told me I'd have to take what I wanted then because tomorrow would be too late.

The fish were on their spewing migration and they were in a hurry about it. So, instead of one trip, I made two.

It was four days later when a lady who worked for the airline asked me to drop by. I dropped everything. When I arrived I told her that I was ready to ship and that I had them in a local freezer.

Her comeback was, "Luther sent you a message. He told me to say this in his exact words, okay?!" she replied.

"Sure. go ahead!" I said, "Say it in his exact words."

"He said, 'Fuck Walter Noden and his damn white fish!' "

I was in shock. She went on to explain that she found out that he had the fish in a commercial freezer in Anchorage and when he went to get a sample, he had accidentally locked himself in it. Evidently, some time had passed before he was found in the freezer. He was mad as hell, having nearly frozen to death.

The idea didn't go completely to hell. I gave the fish to the local Catholic school. I must ask, was my mistake an answer to a prayer?

Liar

I used the Aeroncia Sedan for everything that would fit through its door. For a prospecting and fishing trip camper. With the back seat removed, it made a roomy two-person sleeping quarters. Everything from fresh salmon to dog teams was flown in it.

I always told people, "Just bring it! If it fits through the door, I'll fly it."

There was a time when I had to refuse.

There was this guy who came to see me.

"Walt, I want you to take my girlfriend and me on a pleasure trip for a couple of hours. How much do you charge?"

I told him my hourly rate. I told him it was no less than one half-hour.

"Okay," he said. "I want two hours, but I want privacy."

"What do you mean?" I asked.

"I want a canvas divider between your area and ours."

I asked him to explain and he did.

"NO! Absolutely not!" I said.

"I'll pay double." the guy replied.

"I said NO!"

"I'll pay triple!" he pressed on.

"Dammit! I have to say no! My friends will hear about this and call me *Noden's Flying Playhouse Airlines*," I replied.

I did stick to my "NO."

I didn't care too much about everyone in our small town hearing about it. But my wife would surely be one of the first to hear—but for triple pay??!!

87

Aeronicia Champ—$800

We were living in Anchorage, Alaska, when I read this ad in the *Anchorage Times*.

AERONCIA CHAMP—$800

I called and asked how bad the damage was.

"There's no damage," the owner said.

"Well, you made a mistake in your ad. You have it for sale for eight hundred dollars," I pointed out.

"No, I didn't make a mistake. That's my price," he replied.

"What happened?" I asked.

"Well, it's frozen in a lake behind Toyonak Village with just the wing tips showing. If you bring me eight hundred right now, it's yours," the owner said.

I had the money, so I brought it to him.

When I arrived at his place, I showed him the eight hundred.

"I'll put this on your table. Please tell me the whole story before you pick it up," I told him.

"All right," he said. I went moose hunting just after freeze-up. I landed on that damn lake to get that moose. When I slowed down, the damn thing fell through the ice. My partner and I just barely got out of that plane. The next day I had a friend take me over and we found the plane under the ice with just the wingtip showing. I got home and got mad about the situation all over again, so I put an ad in the paper for eight hundred. Here's the title and the headache that goes with it!"

A very, very good friend of mine, Don, had access

to a plane. So, we went out to the lake to see just how bad it was. We had no trouble finding it, because the owner had marked the place with a spruce tree limb. The plane was frozen in, but it wasn't as bad as the guy thought.

That evening Don and I talked about salvaging it. Things like, do it now by chopping ice, or in the summer with a diver.

During this conversation, I noticed Danny, my son, acting like he had something to say.

"Dan, you just got out of high school and want something to do. So, if you're going to help us get that damn thing out, say what's on your mind," I said.

"Dad, I helped a guy one time to work on his outboard motor. He made me chop a hole in the ice and he started the kicker in the hole. When he was through working on that kicker, I noticed that the propeller had made that ice hole a lot bigger," Danny replied.

Don was looking at me with a big smile, and it was catching. I turned to Danny with a great big grin. "Dan Doc from Queenahak, you just made yourself the head man of the frozen-in-the-lake salvagers."

The first thing we did find was a long, but small diameter, spruce tree. We stuck it through the ice and pushed it all the way to the bottom at an angle so, that it would freeze in for our hoist.

Don had borrowed two small three-horsepowered outboards. We built two small sledges. They were made out of two by fours, light plywood, and wood screws.

This idea worked like a charm. The prop-wash

melted the ice behind and around the prop. As the ice melted behind the prop and under its sledge, the whole thing moved itself to melt more ice.

Don and I were working, so that left the chief of the salvagers, Dan, and his radio at the out camp permanently. He was there to keep the outboards running and to make sure the sleds did not freeze in the ice. We didn't have problems with the sleds freezing in the ice, probably due to the mild spring weather and the constant vibration from the outboards. Don would fly over to camp there at night.

About the third or fourth day, we had the plane floating on the lake from the buoyancy of the ice in the fuselage and cabin. Our scrounger found a water pump and a piece of fire hose. Dan tied the nozzle in different spots inside the fuselage to melt this ice as he lifted it a little at a time with the block and tackle we had rigged.

When it came to the engine, we were all in agreement. Since it was covered with fresh, clean water, we'd just let it dry out good and change the oil.

I took the mags to Anchorage because we wanted them good and dry before they were fired. I blew all the water from them with an air hose and put them in an open oven on low heat. The next morning I bought two condensers; and that was just to say that I did something.

The plane started on the second propping. Don was in it and when he taxied out onto the lake, I thought he intended to taxi it to make sure the engine was running okay and then come back. NO! He just took off for Anchorage. He did come back before night-fall with a bigger plane to pick us up.

Don and my daughter Rose, who happened to be his wife, flew the plane to New York and back to Anchorage.

One guy came up to me and asked, "You know Don and Rose are flying to New York?"

"Yeah. He got my daughter. He got my plane. I think I'll hide my canoe. It's the only thing I got left!"

Piper Family Cruiser

I had an old Piper Family Cruiser. The few "horses" it had when new were half-dead when I got it.

I was using it on skis to pick up a prospector. It was white-out conditions where the King Salmon met the Nushigak River. Thankfully I could see enough to land on the snow. The guy was all ready to go, so we started to load his gear. I was about to tell him that we had more than enough, when he showed me one more sack. I picked it up to feel the weight of it. I was sure, by the weight of it and the plain rock look, that it was just some dark sedimentary rock.

"No, we can't take it. It's just a sack of rocks," I told him.

"It could be coalumbite," he replied.

We argued about it until I got tired of it and let him bring it aboard. I should have said, "You or the rock. Take your pick."

I had set down in a clearing surrounded by tall

spruces on take off. I miscalculated the size of the clearing because of the white out.

The trees were suddenly coming at me and I made mistake number two. Instead of going straight into the trees and possibly having a salvageable plane, I tried to turn and it stalled out. The plane went into deep, powdery snow, nose first, folding the wings back.

We had to crawl out through the tail end and cut through the fabric with my ax to get out. There wasn't a scratch on either one of us. I stomped out a spot to sit down in the snow. I told the prospector to do likewise.

"You bastard! You tried to kill me!" he said.

He tried to run through the snow, so I'd go and drag him back. He did it about three times.

After I got him settled down a bit, I crawled into the plane and got my rations and ax. Then I chopped out the radio, antenna, and the battery.

I hung the antenna in a tree and called King Salmon. I don't know what I was expecting, but to my surprise, the radio worked. King Salmon called right back. They told me that they would call Army rescue and that I was to stay on that channel.

Fifteen minutes passed and the Army called to say that they'd fly overhead inside one and a half hours. They were going to drop survival rations.

That was when I proved that not only was I a dirty bastard but also a stupid one at that. I asked them to call a party in Dillingham to send a plane to come get us. If I would have let them do it their way, I could have gotten enough sleeping bags and food items to last me a lifetime.

It was towards spring with long days and we were home that evening. My only excuse for my stupidity was that I was tired. The flying hours in spring and summer are long and it was fatigue that caused me to act as I did. The plane is still up on that mountain with George's fifty pounds of "cooloombite!"

Other Stories

Outhouse

I became friends with a bachelor at one of the villages I traveled to. One time I went to his house, I walked outdoors to go to his outhouse (no sewers at this village). It was gone, and I couldn't find any outhouse.

I went and asked, "What the hell you do with your outhouse?"

"Oh! Walt, I got a new thing. It burns the stuff, works beautiful, and it all just goes up the stack, no more carrying shit."

On my next trip to his village, the honey bucket was back in. I asked, "What the heck happened to your new thing?"

"Oh! The damn neighbors burned it down. The damn idiots! I found out that the neighbors couldn't stand the thing. It stunk up the whole neighborhood and they just went there, ran over it with a bulldozer, then burned the whole thing. I couldn't do a damn thing about it. I told them I was moving from the neighborhood."

"What'd they say?" I asked. "They said, 'thank you, we don't need no shit stinking neighbor.' I said I was going to sue."

"What then?" I asked.

"They said, 'Go right ahead, there's two of us in the village council and one of us is the judge.' "

Von at a Time

A group of old prospectors and miners got themselves pretty tipsy during a wake for one of theirs. Since no one could be found to do it, the next day during the burial one of them was reading from the Book. As the coffin was being lowered with ropes by four of the more stable ones, one of them fell in along with the coffin. The reader remarked, "Von at a time now, boys! Von at a time!"

Grave-Gamble

I was at Saint Lawrence Island on a short job. The island village of Gamble sets right next to a high mountain ridge. One Sunday, it was so nice and sunny that I decided to climb up the mountain a ways. I was probably about three hundred feet up the mountainside and sat down on the end of a wooden box that was showing out of the large and small boulders on the mountainside. I surmised it was something the Army had left.

I was watching a fox and he'd go from boulder to boulder to observe me. I squirmed my butt on this box to observe him in return. I was moving myself on the end of the box; the end fell off. When I looked I saw human bones. I quickly put the end back, put some smaller boulders against it, and turned around to get the heck out of where I didn't belong. My first steps away was the first and only time I ever had that unexplainable feeling that went down my spine. I turned around and went a little ways, getting down the mountain going backwards.

The next day at the powerhouse where I was doing a repair job, I told the maintenance man about my mountainside encounter. He told me that years ago, the old people didn't have the tools to go through the hard ground anywhere near the village, so they laid their people to rest on the mountainside among the boulders.

I apologized to him for my mistake. He said, "You and I don't have to say anything right now. This is your second trip here. If you make more trips here and get older, I'll make you join the village and put you up there too!

Lake Sleep

A friend and I were dropped off at a small lake for an overnight moose hunt. When we unrolled our tent, we found the mice had chewed it full of holes. We set it up anyway, saying it would keep some of the wind out and we'd be okay, only if it didn't rain.

I awoke in pouring rain. My bag was soaking wet and my friend was in the same condition. We started our two-burner Coleman to help keep warm and to make coffee. My friend started a conversation.

"Hey, you know, I was told the water in these lakes stay at forty degrees winter and summer."

I said, "I guess it's got to be above thirty-two degrees or the water would freeze."

Next I know he was putting on his shoes.

"It's no use to put your shoes on," I told him. "They're just as wet as everything else and you can't light a campfire in this weather."

His final sounding remark was, "I'm not lighting no fire. I'm going out to get in the lake water. It's warmer than this and can't be any more wet."

Ben's New Boat

There wasn't a fish in the whole bay and not one on my barge the *Mink*. When Ben came alongside with his new boat, one thing led to another, and it came to how fast his new boat was.

He said, "Come, I'll show you."

When he headed for Dillingham, the main town in the area, I figured out what the visit was about. He had a new boat, but his wallet was old and empty, and he wanted a drink.

On the way back to my barge from Dillingham with our two bottles, I had to go and the only thing he had "going for that" was an open five-gallon bucket. He was bringing me the paper, with the boat still at full throttle and no one at the wheel, when we hit a half-sunk tundra turf. Everything went forward in a hurry. Ben went against the binnacle, me and the shit bucket went against the pilothouse.

When we got to the barge where my wife was the cook, bottle washer, tallyman, and boss, she started with, "Where you been? What? You smell, get out! You smell! Just get out of this galley. I'll bring you clothes."

She just wouldn't stop saying, "What did you do?"

I got half mad and said, "Please get me something to change into. Someday I'll write you a letter and tell you all about it."

You waited a few years for this, didn't you, Flo?

Boat-Prop

There was some work to be done on the propeller shaft on my fish boat. I beached the boat at a desirable tidal beach to remove the shaft. As we pulled the shaft out, I remarked to my helper, "I sure been having problems with this damn boat lately. Now, all I have to do is forget to plug that shaft hole before the next tide, then I'll have the engine to repair too."

Early the next morning there was a knock at the door. To my "good morning," the kid said, "They told me to tell you *your* boat is sunk."

Seal Gut Window

At the end of the day at one of the villages, the maintenance man asked me to supper at his home. When we arrived there, I thought it was a barrabra, but inside it was a one-room plywood house with a wood floor.

He had built the thing of plywood and covered it with dirt. Made it look the same and as warm as a drift wood and dirt barrabra. It had a seal-gut window through the roof such as the barrabras used.

There were no chairs and we had supper of boiled seal, sitting cross-legged on the floor, in a circle. After dinner he asked if I'd like an after-dinner drink. I was just beginning my "Why sure, you bet" words when he rolls out one of the bundles that laid against the wall (they were rolled-up bedding) and set the full quart of the better whiskeys on the floor with glasses. We drank scotch, sitting cross-legged on the wood floor with the moonlight from a seal-gut window.

Fishing Trip

One of my stupid trades, I acquired a small, flat-bottomed wooden cabin cruiser. I talked my wife Florence into going on a fishing trip in that thing.

We were newly wed and had our first baby. Florence didn't have a portable crib or anything to keep the baby in. She found an oblong galvanized tin tub. These oblong tubs were used in our part of Alaska for everything imaginable, like fish crating, washing, and, in our case, a baby crib.

We were going up the Wood River, a branch of the Nushagak in the Bristol Bay area. The damn vessel leaked so bad that we had to take turns bailing. We were to the stage where the argument was, "who bailed the most"; and that got pretty heavy.

We saw this other boat anchored and cast fishing. To take a rest from bailing, we decided to tie up to them and borrow their pump. We got alongside and found out it was a ship's shore boat. Aboard were four young sailors. They were off a Coast Guard boat anchored near Dillingham. When we got alongside, one of the guys looked in our boat, saw our baby afloat in her tub, and remarked, "You have a little water aboard, but I guess y'all are used to it."

Tom and the Cat

Tommy Wong was a cook at a salmon cannery where I worked. There was about eight of us having a late evening snack in the dining room part of the kitchen/dining room complex. I happened to look into the kitchen area and saw a cat standing inside a good-sized tub eating something. I motioned for Tommy, the cook, and pointed toward the cat and tub operation. I followed when Tommy ran in there with a gunny sack. He threw in a full one-gallon can off the shelf, grabbed the cat, put the cat in the sack with the can, and ran through the back door. I followed him down to the nearby slough; all the while he was singing some kind of Chinese war chant. When the sack hit the water, there was an emphatic end to his chant.

The next day one of the cannery workers, Angie, told me her cat was missing and asked if I had seen it. I truthfully answered, "No, Angle, I haven't seen your cat TODAY!"

Tommy Wong's Sign

At the time of this instance, there were two types of uses the gillnets had in Bristol Bay. One was the drift net attached to a drifting boat with a number. The other was a set-net, which is a net tied to the beach at the high-tide level with a stake with the owner's name and assigned number of the fishermen written on it.

When the Fish and Game made their check of the "set-netters," they came to Tommy Wong's set-net stake and asked him where his stake was. Tommy pointed to a sign with Chinese writing on it. "There, my name-numba!"

Rat Trap

I had a week's work in one of the towns in southeast Alaska. I was issued a pickup truck. The truck was not to be used after working hours.

The bar where I liked to go to had a warehouse attached in back. I would park the pickup in back, out of sight, and go through the warehouse to the bar. It was their liquor storehouse and full of boxes except for a hand-truck alley.

As I walked through the alley between the liquor boxes, I'd see this plate in the alley with what looked like flour in it. Once, I stepped on it and spilled the contents on the floor.

I told the bartender, "You know that plate in the hall with what looks like flour in it? Well, I, split it—what is it?"

He said "Yeah, Walt, that's our new style rat trap. We mix flour and cement together, and when the rats eat it, they turn hard as a rock."

I said, "You sure it's working? I haven't seen any hard-as-a-rock rats back there."

He said, "No, it hasn't worked so good. We might have to go back to our old system."

"Yeah?" I said, "What's your old system?"

"Oh! We go downtown, find an old wino we know, give him a bottle and a broken pool cue, and when he sees a rat, he just knocks him on the head."

Sandpaper Note

There was no central power system in our small village. Usually, three or four houses would join together to operate a small, engine-driven power plant. There were three of us in our power co-op.

One day, we decided to do some much-needed maintenance on our plant. Our project went along fine until our beer supply ran out. The vote was two to one that Walt buy the beer. He said his credit had run out at the store. Boise's credit was good, so he said he'd write a note to the store.

The only piece of writing material we could find was a piece of sandpaper. Boise wrote the note on the back of the sandpaper and Walt took off to the store.

Walt soon came back empty handed and a little cranky.

I asked, "What went wrong? Store closed?"

"NO! He kicked me out and gave me the note back. I took the note. On the back of the sandpaper, it read, *'Please give Walt a case of beer and charge to me. If you don't want to give him the beer, wipe your ass on this. Boise.'* "

Work on Furnace

One of the guys came in late for the evening gathering at the local emporium. He was telling the guys how long and hard he worked that day on his mother's furnace. He was waiting for his second glass when a kid came running in yelling, "Butch, your mom's house is on fire"!

Native Spear

I was doing a job in a native village in southeast Alaska. The king salmon run was in full swing and I wanted one to take home. I'd be on my way home late the next day, so I borrowed a fishing pole from the teacher and was casting. The "kings" didn't pay any attention to my hook whatsoever. I could see them in the clear stream.

It wasn't long before one of the locals came wading to me with a large, native, spear.

He said, "Don't use that thing. They throw with that piece of string; it don't catch nothing. Besides that, when you use that thing, Game Warden's come asking you for fish license." Then he waved that big, native spear and said, "But when you use this kind, he don't come ask you for no damn license!"

DWI

An old native friend of mine went before the local judge for Driving While Intoxicated (DWI). The judge asked the interpreter to tell him he was charged with DWI. The interpreter told the judge that he could not relay his request in his exact wording.

The judge told the interpreter to try to explain the reason for his arrest the best he could. After some conversation in the Alaskan native language, the interpreter told the judge, "Your Honor—he said he does not drink when he's driving. He stop, take a drink, then he drive."

The case was dismissed. The interpreter told me the judge told him, "Don't ever come here with another story like that again because *you'll* be the one thrown in jail!"

Miner in Court

Miners and prospectors, during what's referred to as the "old days," lived off the land. One miner was in court for killing over his limit for moose.

The judge said, "You are charged with killing more than one moose. We have six freshly killed moose legs as evidence. What have you to say in your behalf?"

"I admit I have six moose legs, Your Honor, but I want to know if you have a law that says a moose can't have six legs?"

He was asked to leave the courtroom and to take his friends, who were the audience, with him.

Waterbed Wine

I became very good friends with one of the teachers in northwestern Alaska. On one of my trips, I stopped at his home. In fact, the village guys told me he asked me to be sure and stop by.

As soon as I got to his house, the first thing he said was "Walt, please come and look."

He led me to a small room part of the building. He said, "Look! Look at this," pointing at a small waterbed, which was the only thing in the room.

"Ya, I see. It's a nice small waterbed."

"No, no! Walt, it's a wine cask! I'll show you."

He ran into the kitchen and came back with a pitcher full.

He filled two glasses, handed me one, and said, "Now taste this and tell me what you think."

I told him what I thought.

Since that time I've told my friends—drinking friends and sober ones—that it is the best wine I ever drank. He told me how this wine business all started.

The people that lived there before him left the one-man waterbed. He got to looking at it, found it had an electric heater, temperature controls, and a water drain valve.

He said, "Walt, since I make my own wine and am a chemist besides, it didn't take me to long to start this waterbed wine making business. The whole thing came together as planned. Walt, the water here is pure rainwater. The prunes and raisins I use are perfect, and I can keep control of the fermenting temperature. The bed has a water temperature control, and it also has a nice waterproof liner. If you're going to ask why the wine doesn't taste like the inside of a waterbed or a pair of boots, I'll tell you. The liner is made of plastic that does not taint the wine."

As we were saying our good-byes the next day, he said, "Walt, you now have one accomplishment you can be proud of—you are one of the only one of two people on this earth who have been drunk on waterbed wine!"

Alaska Native Wild Man, Klutak

The first story I heard about Klutak was the one my mother told me. Her mother told her the story.

Klutak came to a village. He was very demanding. He demanded the best sod hut, the best food, the best clothes made from the finest skins, the youngest and prettiest maidens.

The village elders decided something had to be done. They talked about this in council for some time. One day, an old lady approached the council. She told them that her mother told her about the same kind of bad man and how they had done away with him.

The council asked her to take care of the man. In other words, to get rid of the guy her own way. She would take care of Klutak's demise, then the council would repay her in their way, and not another word would be said about it.

The old woman knew that the man gulped his food down in large chunks. She fixed him a nice big meal of meat with springy pieces of wood wrapped in it. When the meat was digested, the springy boards would puncture his stomach.

It was just a few days later that Klutak was found dead in his barrabra.

The last time I heard about Klutak in my area, Bristol Bay, was when he was blamed for a killing at a cabin near the head of the Nushagak River, in the Bristol Bay area of Alaska. He was blamed for splitting a trapper's head open with an ax.

Klutak was a "Village Alaska" fall guy. Klutak got

the blame for any unsolvable killings or thefts. Alaskan villages didn't have law enforcement, such as police. Whenever there was a major crime, the only thing that the village council could do to put the crime to rest was say, "Klutak did it!"

Klutak disappeared when Alaska towns and villages began to have state and federal police. If Klutak cracked someone's head open today, the last thing he would remember was sitting in a high-powered chair.

In the Lower 48, they had Bigfoot. In Alaska the one I heard of made big tracks in the snow. When he was seen, he just took off and could not be caught or seen again.

Bigfoot was seen only once in Alaska that I know of. One of my friends told me about the time he heard about Bigfoot. He was in a bar in this town and some guys were talking about seeing Bigfoot. They said they were jumping their snow travelers next to the graveyard where the small wavy hills were. They saw this big guy, really big, black and furry. When they went toward him, he took off. They chased him but couldn't catch him. All they could see was great big furry feet. He got away from them when he got to an area where there wasn't much snow. They just had to give up the chase and go have a drink instead.

At this same bar the next day, I listened to three native guys talking at a table. One of them was saying, "You know, guys around here are getting too tough! The other day I was up in the graveyard, stealing crosses for my firewood, and three snow travelers tried to run me over.

109

"I ran like hell and got away from them. They almost caught me because I had my big heavy fur mukluks on and couldn't run very fast. You guys know, when mukluks are new, the fur on the sole makes it hard to run on snow. Besides that, I had my big wolf fur coat on."

Red and His Dog

Red lived in a log cabin about a mile and a half from downtown Dillingham. He had his repair shop there for radio and anything electrical that was sent to him for repair. His home, a log cabin about 12' X 15' had no electricity. He used a coal/oil lamp. Everyone in town who could afford it had a small gasoline power plant.

Red had just a small log cabin with enough room for a stove to make a cup of coffee. I don't know how that dog moved in with Red, but Red and that dog lived together.

Red would walk to town, dragging his wagon and tools behind, or drag a sled in winter. That dog followed him. He finally obtained a small sheet metal wagon and that dog followed Red as he pulled the wagon.

One day, Red told me it was his lucky day.

"How's that Red?"

"Well, you see, one of my native customers paid me in dog food. I calculated that the weight of my dog was one-fifth of your huskies, so if your huskies live on one fish a day, my dog would live for five days per fish."

I didn't think to tell him that we also feed our dogs cooked food that consisted of tallow (cannery cook-houses used frying oil) and rolled oats or rice brought from the canneries when they left for the winter. They didn't want some items laying over the winter and only asked a token payment.

Another thing, the fish Red got came from a village 150 miles up river, and these fish had lost most of their fat getting up river. It may have been a month or close to two months later when I met Red dragging his wagon.

I asked, "What happened to your dog?"

"Oh, the beast up and died on me!"

Red and the Pussycat

Another time, Red came to me and asked, "Walt, do you have a stray cat I could borrow?"

"No, Red, I don't have any stray cats. If I did you could have all I have. What's this all about, Red?" I asked.

"Oh! You see, Walt, I have this job at the airport and I need a cat."

"Oh, I see, you need a bulldozer?"

"No! No! I need a feline type of cat," he replied.

"Okay, Red, let's go through this again. You have a job at the airport and you want a cat to give you a hand, right?"

"Yes, the airport's fourteen landing lights are out on the west side. I want to make a temporary connection. If I could get this cat to pull a piece of twine to the other side through one of the culverts, I'd have it made.

"You see, Walt, earlier I had it made. I had the string and the cat, the whole mess, but I lost the string along with the pussy, he just took off on me. I had the whole rig set up. The cat was harnessed to the string, but no matter what I did, the damn beast didn't want to start across that culvert. He just refused to go. But I came up with a solution. I got me a good-sized little bunch of this dried grass around here, tied the grass to his tail, put my ball of string in a well-placed coffee can. I pointed the cat in the right direction and lit fire to the grass. You should have seen that pussy go! I was so amazed at the speed of that pussy that I forgot to hang on to my end of the string. Now I'm desperate for another cat and ball of string!"

"Well," I said, "if you'll tell me how the rest of the day went, I'll buy you a drink tonight. Don't give up, Red, you still have the empty coffee can to start with. You just need another pussy!"

Red and Queen

When the U.S. Signal Corps put in their transcender in Kanakanak, they had a radio-tech with them. When the job was done and he was to leave, he quit his job to stay in the area. When I asked him why, he said, "I fell in love with your country and your people and I'm staying."

I'll call him "Red." We became very good friends. I had a small mechanical shop in Dillingham, and Red would borrow a tool or something else from my shop every so often. Red, when he was called to do a job, considered it done. He didn't tell the customer to order this or that part. Instead he got the thing running using parts from discarded radios and electrical appliances people gave him.

The cannery I flew for had a barge that had to go to Seattle for the winter. When they were all ready for the barge to leave, the radar went flop. There were no parts or any way to make the thing work.

They asked me if I could find someone to fix it. I told them I'd find them the best man in Alaska. I brought Red down there. I told the captain he'd have to supply the beer for Red or I'd bring the beer. They said, "Don't worry. We have all he'd want."

It was early the next morning when I brought Red there. Towards late evening I stopped by at the cannery. The captain knew whose plane was landing and met me at the airstrip.

He said, "Damn you, Noden! Your man has my damn radar all to pieces and scattered from here to hell. I trusted you, Walt. I didn't think you'd do that to me! He already had drunk over a case of beer! What do we do now?"

I said, "Just feed him beer and leave him alone. I'll come tomorrow late and pick him up. You have two days before you leave. If he don't fix it by then, I'll find you a radar some place."

When I went there late the next day, the captain came running to me and said, "How did he do it? He put all that wire and crap all together and it works."

I asked, "Where is he?"

"Oh, he'll stay here tonight and have a drink. He'll get double pay and you too! Tomorrow you pick him up."

The Cab Ride

One of my first trips out of the Bristol Bay area in Alaska was to Seattle. I was paying that damn smart cabbie, when he asked me, "What part of Bristol Bay you come from?"

My answer was, "How'd you know I come from Bristol Bay?"

He said "Because everyone who pays me five bucks to take him around the corner come from Bristol Bay!"

One Quart

One of my friends had a drinking problem. His wife was trying to get him to slow down. She quit giving him money, but he got his bottle somehow.

She asked me to find out and promised not to tell him I squealed. I wanted to know in case it happened to me. I asked him how he did it, and in the same breath, I assured him my mouth was shut tight.

He said, "Walt, you see that garden hose coiled up on the holder?"

"Yeah, sure. It's nicely coiled on that garden hose holder, so what?"

"You see, I'm the gardener for the family—she doesn't touch that hose and she likes it that way. I like it that way too because I know what's in that hose—it holds one quart of good booze."

I just wrote about it. I didn't squeal. Would you?

Crawling Drunk

On one of my first visits to jail, I woke up on the iron cot. From there I was escorted before the judge.

The judge picked up my citation, and read it. He read, "When first observed, subject was attempting to crawl to his car; when questioned, subject repeatedly told the officer, fuck you."

The judge looked at me, riffled through his papers, looked at me again, and said, "You don't belong here, case dismissed" and he banged his hammer on his table.

I was so startled and dumbfounded that I didn't feel the tug on my shirt from the young attorney, and friend of mine. When he finally got me out, he said, "Next time one of those guys throw you out of court, please get the hell out!"

Gill O

I had a job that entailed travel to Alaskan native villages to repair diesel electric power plants.

Every village had all the parts needed to repair their power plants. There was one area that stored their parts in a larger town that I went to for parts, for the surrounding villages. I went to the parts department and asked for a parts manual for a particular power plant. The guy said they didn't have parts manuals. He said, "Just go ask Gill and give him your parts list. He'll get them for you."

I followed Gill to the warehouse with my long list of parts for three different power plants.

I said, "Gill, I watched you do that. Please tell me I'm not going cuckoo!

He said, "No! No! I'm the cuckoo! Those doctors and professor take me out stateside and said I have photographic memory. I can read that book once and remember everything in it."

Kavalilla

I landed my Super-Cub on a small mountain hill. It wasn't a hill or a small mountain. I guess it was in between.

Kavalilla was an elderly native man. I wanted him to tell me where he'd been in this part of the drainage and what, if any, minerals he'd found. I'd taken the bottom cushions from the plane and we sat on them and he told his story.

"I was one of the young boys chosen for this training trip. We carried the same survival gear as everyone else. At camp time we gathered the wood for the cook fire, carried water, and did whatever else the elders wanted." He said, "We made our main camp close to the head of this King Salmon River we're looking at now. Not here, but farther up."

"The people gathered together right about here. They traveled from the Kuskokwim area, Togiak, Nushagak, Naknek, Illiamna Lake and Kiniak. He emphasized the last mentioned name.

He made sure I understood that these people carried and paddled their two place canoes from the Kenai area to this meeting place—through mountains, swamps, and what else besides mosquitoes.

When I asked him to tell me more, he said, "Start you white-man fly canoe; let's go. I feel itchy like mosquitoes bite me—even no mosquitoes!"

Tribal House

During my work as traveling Diesel Electric Power Plants mechanic, I became well acquainted with village people and council members of one of the outlying villages.

During one of my trips to this village, I was told, that since I could become a guest member on my next visit to the village, I should go to the Tribal House to see their house totems.

This building had a wide shelf along each side and, also, at the middle area where each family kept their artifacts. There were family totems and other family artifacts. There were also "Village Artifacts." One of these was, to me, very noticeable.

I said, "Steve, what is that? It sure looks like blond hair."

"Yes it is, wait! I'll tell you first, it's very old—it's a human scalp!" He said, "I'll tell you the way it was told to me!

"Many, many years ago, a sailing ship came to our village to rob our fur. This captain stole one of the young maidens, then raped and killed her. The people got together and asked the medicine man what they could do.

"The medicine man told them what he would see happen! The ship would decide to leave, then they would stop the ship and captain would go into the woods out in the bay, there you warriors wait for him and take his scalp.

"Sure enough, the ship on its way out became becalmed. When the ship stopped, the largest eagle in the whole world circled the ship and landed abreast of the ship in the highest tree.

"The captain wanted that big eagle, launched a long boat, and ran in the woods to get it. That's when they got the big scalp."

Steve said, "Walt, take another good look at that blond scalp—then believe what you want—none of us here were not born that long ago and we all same way—we each believe or not—our choice; you to have a choice believe the old stories or not—your choice!"

Jon Wallapusa

During the sailboat fishing times, the "BS" about what had happened during the fishing season started after we put our cannery-owned boats away for the season.

This was the time I first heard about Jon Wallapusa.

This man had walked up the Nushagak River from near its mouth at Creek Cannery to its head at Koligallek, about 150 miles.

He started his walk during the early spring, just before the summer salmon-fishing season. This was during the most intense of our mosquito season and also, the time of high waters in the swamps, rivers, and streams.

Later that fall, I ran into him in Dillingham and invited him to my home for a visit. My wife Florence asked him, "Jon, I heard you walked all the way from Creek-Cannery to the head of the Nushagak—why"?

He said, "Florence, I've been to quite a few different places on this earth, but I've never meet a friendlier people. I wanted to know your land and see it as your people did. What better way than to walk through it, live in it, and with it as your people did."

I talked with him at that time.

"Jon, I'd like to ask a little bit about your trip, okay? What did you take along for clothes and food?" I asked.

"I had a pair of native-make knee boots, made from seal and caribou hide. For clothes I had a light raincoat and a wool blanket. For food I had some tea, a tin cup and saucer, salt and matches. I rolled this all in a light canvas. I, also, had enough food to last for the first few days of the trip."

He said his main meat was ground squirrel that he caught with a snare. He explained that vegetable and greens were no problem because the greens were already starting their new summer growth. The wild root was very good.

He told Florence that he found her country could easily compare to any other place on earth, mostly because her people were so very friendly.

Henry O'Yea

The platinum mine at Good News was, at one time, the largest producer of platinum in the U.S. Two native men—Henry O'Yea and another native man—made the initial discovery.

Here is what Henry told me about finding the platinum mine at Good News Bay.

"My native friend tell me he find gold and heavy black stuff—heavy like gold. Him and me go look. I don't know what the black rock is, and after we talk long time, I tell him we have to go see white man. After long time we talk about who is smartest white man; my partner say maybe schoolteacher is smartest.

"He say, one time, he see schoolteacher write paper for other white man. Next day, we go see schoolteacher. We tell him he be our partner if he help us find out what that black rock with the gold is. Next day, school teacher say he don't know what black stuff is, and we have to find other white man to help us and make him partner too.

"Now we got two white men partners. The next day, our two white men make partner with other white man with dog team to take gold and black stuff to post office with dog team. Our schoolteacher partner say we have to wait for letter. We wait long time.

"When letter come, it come with tell-o-gram and tell-o-gram come with dog team. Tell-o-gram say yellow stuff gold—black stuff platinum. Our white man partner say we have lots of money. And then our partner say we go outside—I think 'Sansisco'—get more money.

"We, all of us go, me and my pat-bier and our three white man partner. We, all of us, have lots of money. We go to big eat house every day and we sleep with different white man's women every nighttime.

"When we get home, our partner say we put our money saving. My partner, he don't want saving. I put mine, some of it, for save.

"Walter, I take little from saving all the time and lend my partner some because he spend all his money—no saving."

Mountain Story

We were sitting on top of a small hill-mountain. Too large to be a hill and too small to be a mountain.

An old native friend and I came here in my *Piper Super-Cub* that was parked at the base of this small mountain. We were on a prospecting trip.

He wanted to get to this vantage point so he could see the country as he saw it during his child-manhood days.

First "Cuv" pointed to the spot where "That white man kill other white man—gold there."

Then he told me a story.

He told me he was with the grown-ups for a young boys training trip. He said when he was old enough, he went with the elders to a meeting of the people in this area. This was a meeting, or large gathering of the people from the surrounding area far and near. People came to this meeting from the Kuskokwim River, up the Togiak River from its mouth, then, also, the Naknek and Illianma Lake area.

My ears perked up when he said the people brought their great big flounder from the Keniak. He explained that each district brought their different foods, such as dried foods and fur to trade for the different types that other villages had.

He said the young boys were tired because they had to keep the campfire burning and the grass mats changed, but they were happy because they got to see the trade goods.

He said, "I'm pretty old now, but I still see that big flounder from over that Keniak place."

Tyki Dog

Our dog, Tyki, was given to the kids by Charlie as a pup. He grew up to be a big friendly dog. Grew up with the kids—slept with them or the chickens (we had six chickens) and pushed the kids off the street, to keep them from getting run over by one of the few cars in town.

He tracked me down when Florence wanted me home. If I was sober when he found me, he would "woff-woff." But if I were other than sober, he would get hold of me by the wrist and lead me home. I had to follow because any resistance would make him bite a little harder and pull.

He was a buddy to every bachelor in town. He got their leftovers and kept them company.

He could come home anytime he wanted. He was big enough to reach the doorknob, that somehow he learned to turn and open, or he'd sleep in the chicken house with the chickens.

I got a note from one of the town preachers. According to the note, I was the worst devil in town. The note went on and on about how much of a hell man I was.

I asked someone in his congregation what this was all about. The guy told me with the straightest face he could ever hold, that it really was not me, it was my dog he was mad at. He had gone out and left his bitch in heat, shut in at home. When he came home, he found my Tyki coupled to his dog in his kitchen.

Tyki Brings a Visitor

It was pretty late in the evening when I heard Tyki's scratch at the door along with some banging on the door. When I opened the door, there was Tyki dog and a friend of mine held by the wrist and blood spitting mad. He had flown in with his Piper Cub from a village about seventy miles away on a booze run when Tyki caught him, and now it was 7:00 P.M. late and dark. When he had cooled down enough for us to drive to his plane to get his load to keep at my place for the night, I said, "Let's stop at Ken's and buy you a spark plug for the plane."

He caught on quick and said, "Yeah—I can't tell them the truth—they'd never believe that one plug went bad and it was too dark by the time I found another spark plug!"

Robert

Robert was like all the rest of the locals. He was a fisherman, trapper, and hunter who lived off the country.

The only difference between him and the others

was he had only one arm. He lost his left arm in an accident, and only a stub remained.

He took me beaver trapping with him one spring. It was 1934 and I was fourteen. It was an enlightening time for me.

First, we built the special sled for the trip. (There were two types of sledges used: the all-around people sled and the wood sled. The people sled was smaller and lighter than the wood sled. These were all the same runner width to be able to stay in the trails that went from village to village, and house to house.)

He made our sled "people sled" weight, but with wider runner width. I asked him, "How come this special sled business?" He said, "Because we'll use it for our boat to come home."

We arrived at the spot where he wanted our camp to be. We unhitched the dogs and turned them loose. He told me not to feed any of them, that they would go to the main camp where they were fed.

I fed, Rusty, my leader. I had Rusty since he was a little newborn pup. I couldn't eat and not feed him.

The dogs did just what Robert said they would do. By the next evening they were gone. Rusty stayed with us.

We made camp on high ground. It must have been about four days before the water was high enough to flood out the beaver.

Then, we took our tent down and used it to cover our sled, and this made a boat, of sorts, that worked fine. The wide sled runners worked good, because they held the alder wood cross pieces and the alder and spruce branches that we used for the bottom walk and freight area.

Beaver live in two types of houses.

There's the bank beaver house. This one is a hollowed-out place in a high bank along side a lake or stream, with the entrance leading to in from under water. The only way you can tell that there's a beaver house in the area is by the cut down alder wood.

The second kind of beaver house is the above-ground house. These are built above the ground on the lake or stream shore.

The above-ground beaver house is, I believe, the best engineered living space ever built by animal or man. Just imagine having a great big orange—cut it in half with the edible meat taken out, then set it open side down on the lake shore, and make an underwater entrance. Make this entrance a maze that only a beaver can negotiate because of time underwater.

The house is built of intertwined alder sticks, and clay from the lake bottom. This clay and short piece of brush makes the beaver home impossible for any animal to destroy, including man. Man could probably break in with a good ax and whole lot of time, but by the time the break in was accomplished, Mr. Beaver and his family would be in their hideout space where they could wait until the intruder left, froze, or starved to death.

By the time we arrived at the main camp, we were shy about two beaver for our two limits, and I had about one dozen muskrats.

The main camp was paradise. There was a steam

126

bath, already cooked food, and people to talk to and fight with.

Piggy-Pig

Piggy-Pig was given to us when first weaned. He lived and grew up with the chickens.

He learned, very early in life, that certain town bachelors were a good food source. He would come home towards evening probably because he'd been put out by the host of the day. This animal was involved in two, to me, memorable instances.

I was cleaning out my cesspool, a large hole about ten-by-ten feet square and full of the stuff that's connected with those things. This native guy came to talk to me and his small boy was standing alongside him. They were both facing toward me and the pool. Then, I saw the pig rambling towards the native boy—poking his nose at the boy's butt to attract attention.

That poor kid must have hit every one of the few floating planks just right because he got across and kept going at full throttle. His dad was right behind him, but he ran around the sewer.

Another time was with the manager of a hardware store. I went to talk to the manager. When I asked for him, I was told that he was not to be disturbed!

I asked, "What's this all about?"

I was told "Walt, don't you know him and the pig have a drink on Saturdays? And he doesn't want to be bothered?

Wood River Belle

The *Wood River Belle* was the first powered barge in Bristol Bay, I believe. The Columbia Ward Packing Company, which had a fish cannery on the Wood River a little above Dillingham, built it as an experiment in hauling fish, using self-propelled barges.

The *Belle* never did haul one fish to the cannery. On its first trip with a load of fish, it got too close to the beach and was grounded. It happened to be at high tide of the largest tide of the summer. The cannery salvaged it, hauled it up on their waves, and that's where it stayed till Albert bought it. By the time Albert got the thing, he couldn't find much use for it either because by that time, bigger and better twin-screw barges were being used. The *Belle* was good to me. I used it with mostly family crew. We got the small hauling jobs. Had a contract to haul raw fish to a small cannery, just the small stuff no one else wanted.

My crew on the *Belle* was family. My wife, Florence. was mate, engineer, and cook. Fred, our oldest son, was deck hand. Our oldest daughter, Rose, was home caring for the smaller brothers and sisters. I used it with this crew hauling salmon from the fish catcher boats to a small cannery.

When the cannery was shut down, we used the *Belle* for odd jobs. I had Florence with me on a job to tow three old empty flat scows from Dillingham to a tug that would be at "ships anchorage" near Clark's Point, which was about fifteen miles from Dillingham. Florence, my first mate, cook, and deckhand was with me.

These were old scows that lay at an abandoned cannery for years. One of those damn things sunk during the tow. It slowed us down quite a lot.

We had the tug in sight when we got the call, "Wood River Belle, this is the Hercules. When I answered, the "Hercules" come back was, "We had you in sight for some time. Will you be alongside on this tide?" My comeback: "Hercules, this is the Wood River Belle. Yes, alongside about high tide."

When we got to the *Hercules,* Florence was on deck to give them a line. The *Hercules* then came on the radio, "Wood River Belle, you'll need more crew on deck. We're passing you a heavy towline." My comeback was,

"Hercules, this is the Wood River Belle. All of my crew is on deck, you see her. Hercules comeback: Wood River Belle, the Hercules, We ask permission for crew to board the "Wood River Belle."

This is the "Wood River Belle, permission granted." When the crew from the Hercules came aboard, I asked Florence to come into the pilot house.

On the way to Dillingham, Florence asked me why I asked her to get off the deck, when all she wanted to do was tell them where things were on deck. I told her, "Florence, you are half owner and mate on this old wreck and when you're on deck, you're the boss. The crew, especially the mate of the *Hercules,* one of the largest tugs in the U.S., would be pretty nervous working under a woman and on top of that, you're an Eskimo Native woman. The coffee didn't come to me until I'd been at the wheel for about an hour and I didn't get any help at Dillingham end to tie-up. I decided I'd better conduct my 'Captain is God' idea with a little more restraint."